T.K.V. DESIKACHAR WITH R. H. CRAVENS

Health, Healing, and Beyond

T.K.V. DESIKACHAR, Krishnamacharya's son and longtime student, is one of the world's foremost teachers of yoga. A renowned authority on the therapeutic uses of yoga, he is the founder of the Krishnamacharya Yoga Mandiram and cofounder of the Krishnamacharya Healing and Yoga Foundation, both of which are located in Chennai, India.

R. H. CRAVENS was born in Salina, Kansas, in 1940. His early career included stints at the Associated Press and Time/Life Books, as well as speechwriting for the United Nations. He had a long affiliation with the fine art photography publisher Aperture, as both a writer and a contributing editor. Cravens died in Albuquerque, New Mexico, in April 2009.

HEALTH, HEALING, and BEYOND

YOGA AND THE LIVING TRADITION OF

T. KRISHNAMACHARYA

T.K.V. DESIKACHAR

WRITTEN WITH R. H. CRAVENS

FOREWORD BY MICHAEL LERNER

AFTERWORD BY C. SUBRAMANIAM

MACMILLAN

First North Point Press edition, 2011
First published in India 2018 by Macmillan
an imprint of Pan Macmillan Publishing India Private Limited
707, Kailash Building
26, K. G. Marg, New Delhi – 110 001
www.panmacmillan.co.in

Pan Macmillan, 20 New Wharf Road, London N1 9RR
Basingstoke and Oxford
Associated companies throughout the world
www.panmacmillan.com

ISBN 978-93-86215-55-0

1 3 5 7 9 8 6 4 2

Printed in India by Thomson Press India Ltd.

This book is dedicated to our mothers:
Shrimati Namagiriamma Krishnamacharya
and Virginia Bergin Cravens

EDITOR'S NOTE

In 1997, during the fiftieth anniversary of Indian Independence, the name of the city of Madras was officially changed to Chennai. Although anachronistic in certain historical references, Chennai is used throughout the text for consistency (with the exception of the University of Madras, the name of which remains unchanged at the time of publication).

All quotations from the *Bhagavad Gita* are from the inspired translations by Juan Mascaró, Penguin Books. Quotations from the *Yoga Sutras of Patanjali* are exclusively drawn from the translation by T.K.V. Desikachar, East-West Books.

Each chapter begins with the words of T. Krishnamacharya.

A map of places visited by Krishnamacharya appears on page 25.

Throughout the text, and particularly in Chapter Two, concerning Vedanta and its leading exponents, we have used dates according to modern Indological research. These do not necessarily accord with traditional Indian teachings, and a satisfactory chronology incorporating and reconciling both viewpoints remains to be worked out.

CONTENTS

FOREWORD

T.K.V. Desikachar is one of the outstanding global authorities on the therapeutic uses of Yoga. He brings a combination of modern empiricism and ancient wisdom, from a most distinguished lineage, to contemporary therapeutic Yoga that helps to bring these practices into the realm of scientific medicine. His teachings have profoundly influenced students of therapeutic Yoga all over the world. His contribution to this field is decisive.

— Michael Lerner
President of Commonweal, a health and environmental research institute in Bolinas, California

INTRODUCTION

"To know the true 'name' of a thing is to evoke it," wrote the Indian mythologist and philosopher Ananda K. Coomaraswamy. It is a principle that lies near the heart of diverse systems of belief and thought. A shaman summons magic in a totemic name, such as "jaguar." Incantatory rites of the priest invoke the Name or names of God. The Platonist reaches toward the Absolute, the ideal in the names of Truth or Justice or Beauty. To know the true name of a thing is to comprehend all that it may signify.

Health, Healing, and Beyond is in large measure the exploration of an ancient wisdom named "Yoga." The word entered the recorded history of mankind in India about two thousand years ago, although the practice of Yoga more likely originated two thousand or more years earlier. Its first mention in the West apparently occurred in 1785 Common Era (CE) with the earliest translation into a European language of the "divine song," the *Bhagavad Gita.* From then through the early twentieth century, Yoga evoked, beyond the borders of the Indian subcontinent, images of exotic adepts with mysterious powers of bodily contortions, able—in some accounts—to exercise superhuman control over time, space, matter, even death.

In the 1930s, a transformation took place that may rank among the milestones in the long, tortuous evolution of human consciousness. A few gifted, persuasive teachers began to travel from India throughout the rest of the world, demonstrating Yogic techniques of physical movement, of controlled breathing, and of mental concentrations. Theirs were not lessons about the supernormal, but of the immediately practical: Yoga could improve bodily health, aid in the healing process, and increase intellectual, creative, and spiritual capacities. Among the most prominent of these teachers were those trained by a single remarkable man, Tirumalai Krishnamacharya. As his son, T.K.V. Desikachar, narrates in the ensuing chapters, Krishnamacharya believed that Yoga was India's greatest gift to the world. Through the efforts of succeeding generations of teachers, many of whom may by now be unfamiliar with Krishnamacharya's name, Yoga is no longer an esoteric practice of the East. It is, in fact, part of the everyday lives of millions of individuals worldwide.

The settings where Yoga is taught are as varied as the needs and interests of its practitioners: universities, community centers, gymnasiums, health spas, hospitals, support groups, and, of course, thousands of specialized schools. It is part of the health regimen of physical exercise and stress management for individuals in every conceivable economic and social class. Yogic techniques are progressively incorporated into healing therapies for respiratory disease, migraines, and chronic back pain, as well as convalescence from injuries, heart attacks, and strokes. Meditative practices of Yoga engage individuals seeking to go beyond the confines of habituated thought and the encumbering demands of materialist societies.

To a considerable extent, Yoga has become associated with a system of techniques involving body movement, breath, and visualization. These are invaluable. They are also only beginnings. Within the profound layers and richnesses of meaning that he discovered in ancient sources, Krishnamacharya revealed unimagined possibilities that Yoga can open for individual human progress.

Krishnamacharya brought the genius of *experienced* language to the teaching of Yoga. If, among many definitions from the original Sanskrit, Yoga means "bringing together," he demonstrated it as a practical matter of consciously realizing the union of body, mind, and spirit.

In another definition, Yoga means "arriving at a place we have not been before." This, Krishnamacharya interpreted literally: human potential is limitless in its capacity for clarity and comprehension and change. As he once wrote, "The relationship between the word and its meaning is eternal, it is not a fabrication."

During a lifetime that spanned more than one hundred years, Krishnamacharya devoted himself with unstinting singleness of purpose to the study, practice, and teaching of Yoga. Because Yoga arises from the wisdom of India, Krishnamacharya determined at a very early age to master this vast body of scientific, philosophical, and religious knowledge. It may fairly be said that, like Goethe of the early nineteenth century, Krishnamacharya in the twentieth century was the last man capable of mastering the entire intellectual heritage of his culture.

Only Krishnamacharya's son, Sri Desikachar, could have assembled the story of the sage's life and work, particularly the final years when he began to introduce revolutionary changes into the physical and spiritual practice of Yoga. For "the living tradition of Krishnamacharya" is as much a matter of experimentation and adaptation as it is of preserving ancient, sometimes long-lost teachings.

Recognized worldwide as a Yoga teacher, Desikachar, a former engineer, was his father's student and colleague for the last thirty years of Krishnamacharya's life. In 1976, Desikachar established a school of Yoga that bears Krishnamacharya's name, in Chennai (formerly Madras), India. Here, in a large building midway along a dusty street in the old Mylapore section of the city, more than two thousand Indians and foreigners each year take part in Yoga therapies, study groups, and teacher training.

The real source of inspiration for teachers and students alike lies at the end of the street, in the corner garden of Desikachar's home. Here, on precisely the spot where Krishnamacharya chose to live out the last two years of his life, is the *sannidhi.* A small, stuccoed, whitewashed building less than twenty feet square, the *sannidhi* is not regarded as a shrine, the usual definition. Krishnamacharya customarily refined and thus redefined words according to their original meanings. For him, *sannidhi* denoted "presence" or "proximity." In this case, the proximity is to a pair of Krishnamacharya's sandals, encased in silver, that have come to rest upon a carved granite pediment.

Although he refused to allow anyone to call him a guru, or even a *Yogi,* during his lifetime, the now semi-legendary sage was always referred to as an *acharya.* No designation could be more accurate. An *acharya* is not simply a wise teacher: he is one who has traveled far and lived what he taught. All that he knows he is said ot have learned at the feet of his own teachers, hence the significance of those well-traveled sandals. And it is in their presence that teachers and students touched by his life's work come, in the words of the great Belgian Yoga teacher Claude Maréchal, "to strengthen their sense of responsibility and to lighten it." Above all, the living tradition of Krishnamacharya is about service to others.

It must in fairness be added, as Desikachar will always emphasize, that there can be no complete and final knowing of the "true" name of Yoga. It is, in another ancient meaning, a "science of the mind." Each mind, as the *acharya* taught, is absolutely unique even as it belongs to universal, eternal Mind. What can be assured is that each individual who seriously undertakes the study of Yoga may discover awaiting, untapped powers of comprehension. The prospect, as Francis Bacon put it more than four centuries ago, is that "the mind can be enlarged, according to its capacity, to the grandeur of the mysteries, and not the mysteries contracted to the narrowness of the mind."

— R. H. Cravens

HEALTH, HEALING, and BEYOND

Scene from the Mahabharata*: Krishna Addressing Arjuna on the Battlefield*

CHAPTER ONE

THE FIRE THAT DISPELS DARKNESS

Whatever place, whatever time, the ancestors have framed Yoga practices to suit them all. Only the attitudes and circumstances of human beings change.

When my father was well into his nineties, I walked into his room one afternoon and found him alone, sound asleep. And he was teaching. Even in sleep his words were clearly distinguishable as he chanted Sanskrit verses in the traditional way that sages of India have always taught their students. On this occasion, as I recall, he was reciting the tale of Valmiki, who was seized by a fit of anger when he witnessed a hunter kill a pair of sacred cranes. In his rage, Valmiki started to lay a curse on the hunter, but when he opened his mouth he instead spoke Mankind's first words of poetry. And this poetry was the beginning of the revelations of the *Ramayana,* the epic poem.

That my father, who was widely known as Professor T. Krishnamacharya, should be teaching in his sleep did not surprise me, although I was deeply moved. In those final years of his long life, I knew he was feeling a great sense of urgency. He had amassed so much knowledge that he alone possessed. He was desperate to pass along as much as possible, knowing that otherwise it would be lost and irrecoverable. Even in dream life, he was never off his teaching.

Krishnamacharya's knowledge was legendary. It included languages, scriptures, theological commentaries, astrology, literature, rhetoric, logic, law, medicine, Vedic chanting, ritual, meditation, music, and much more. He had earned the equivalent of seven Ph.D.'s. His learning would have filled many thousands of pages. It would, that is, if it had all been written down. Much of it he had learned in the oral tradition, from teachers sought out in universities of a bygone era, and in places as distant as temples in tropical southern India and caves in the mountains of Tibet. Virtually all of this scholarly accomplishment he had committed to a memory that remained perfectly accurate into great old age. I was always amazed by it, as were visiting students and scholars. For example, he could quote an exact chapter and verse of the *Mahabharata*, the world's longest epic poem—at 220,000 lines nearly eight times as long as Homer's *Iliad* and *Odyssey* combined.

The knowledge of Krishnamacharya, I should add, might seem not only arcane but also fairly alien to the modern world. He had mastered most of the languages of the Indian subcontinent, and none of the West. Medicine and law as comprehended in the tradition of Krishnamacharya would dismay most of today's practicing physicians and lawyers. His studies had reached back across centuries into the remote past where history fades into myth. This is the realm of the procreators of all Indian science, religion, and philosophy; it is the time of the Buddha, and the age when immortal tales were first written down about fabulous gods, demons, and heroes. Yet, the purpose of my father's erudition was not to preserve the past, but to serve the present and the future.

The astonishing range and variety of his studies all combined toward a single end. This was to place the promise of Yoga at the service of humanity, without regard to age, sex, race, nationality, culture, station in life, belief, or nonbelief.

Krishnamacharya was convinced that Yoga was India's greatest gift to the world. Part of his genius was to use his enormous learning to reshape the ancient wisdom for modern life. In that sense this most orthodox of religious men was also one of the most revolutionary.

He swept aside prohibitions laid down thousands of years ago against the teaching of Yoga to women. To the contrary, he believed that Yoga was even more important for women than for men, in part because it would enhance their health in pregnancy and in giving birth to a healthy child. He also felt that women were the most trustworthy preservers and transmitters of Yogic teaching.

My father was a celebrated healer in his own lifetime. This ability, too, owed much to his willingness to adapt past practices to present needs. He demonstrated the contributions that Yoga could make to physical and mental health—to the prevention of disease and recovery from illness. In many parts of the world his practices are currently being used to help victims of asthma, high blood pressure, diabetes, stroke, digestive disorders, back pain, and a host of other ailments, including mental illnesses and disabilities.

He further proved the value of Yoga in sustaining a lucid, balanced mind in our distracting, stressful, and difficult societies. Toward these ends, he experimented and explored ways to refine Yogic techniques to fit the busy routines of modern life.

Even the healing and sustaining powers of Yoga, however, were only a part of his mission. The true purpose of Krishnamacharya's teaching was to bring Man into contact with something beyond himself, and far greater.

What is Yoga, this gift that promises so much? It is a simple word of vast meaning, subject to many partial understandings and not a few misconceptions.

For many millions of people around the world who practice Yoga, it is a kind of physical exercise that involves prescribed movement and disciplined breathing. This is known as *Hatha* Yoga. For many, Yoga is identified with types of meditation, such as *Raja* Yoga, which reaches toward self-knowledge; or *Kundalini*, the quest for "cosmic energy" and spiritual ecstasy. *Kriya* is concerned with cleansing, which in extreme forms sometimes appears to be self-mutilation. There is also *Tantric* Yoga, popularly characterized by its erotic associations. These and other schools have offshoots and variations that, with more or less fidelity to the true nature of Yoga, have their adherents.

Before offering a very brief summary of the Yoga taught by Krishnamacharya, let me present more fundamental definitions.

"Yoga" is a word from Sanskrit, the original literary and philosophical language of India. The word derives from the root *yuj*, which has two traditional, complementary meanings. The first is "to bring two things together, to meet, to unite." The second meaning: "to converge the mind." The simplest example from daily life is driving a car. We regulate the gas pedal, turn the steering wheel, while simultaneously keeping (it is hoped) our concentration on the traffic and pedestrians around us. Various movements come together and converge with our attention. Champion racing drivers are likely to be among those familiar with moments in a "state of Yoga," even if they might not call it that.

Another meaning may be even more important: "to reach a point we have not reached before." Something that is impossible at this moment becomes possible through Yoga. Today, I sit on the floor and can barely stretch my legs in front of me. After several weeks of practice, I may be able not only to sit erect, but to stretch and bend forward easily, with knees straight, reaching toward my toes. In stages, the impossible becomes possible.

At the deepest level, all of these meanings themselves come together. The source of my father's teaching, and the essence of Yoga, was formulated by the great Indian sage, Patanjali, more than two thousand years ago in this succinct definition:

> *Yoga is the ability to direct the mind exclusively toward an object and sustain that direction without any distractions.*

That "object" can be something as concrete as a work of art, as dynamic as a runner's race, or as abstract as a mathematical formula. It can be as personal and internal to an individual as an exploration of the question "Who am I?" Or it can be as transcendent as being "one with the Lord," whether conceived as a named God or a nameless truth.

There are many, very likely thousands, of texts on Yoga, but the other immortal statement of its meaning occurs in the *Mahabharata.* Like Homer's epic, its theme is a great war, in this case between factions of a divided family descended from an ancient race. About halfway through the poem occurs the most sublime and perhaps the most influential achievement of all Hindu literature, the *Bhagavad Gita.* It is a dialogue between God, in the form of Lord Krishna, and the warrior prince Arjuna.

Arjuna surveys the opposing armies and wishes to withdraw from the struggle, even to die himself, before killing his kinsmen. Krishna awakens in Arjuna the vision of his true self, incapable of death, and calls upon him to fulfill his destiny in the action of Yoga. For Yoga is *action.* Krishna variously describes it as "wisdom in work," as mastery of the "self-willed, impetuous" mind, as "self-harmony," and as the realization that "the God in himself is the same God in all that is." The battlefield portrayed in poetry is, of course, the eternal struggle of Man's striving toward perfection. It is in that sense that Lord Krishna urges Arjuna: "Be one in self-harmony, in Yoga, and arise, great warrior, arise."

Regardless of the religion, revelations require mortal, fallible humans to work out the practical details. This, I believe, was my father's enduring contribution. He was a very practical man, at times even supernaturally so, with an uncanny ability to perceive the human condition. For him, the

Yoga of Patanjali and the *Bhagavad Gita* could be made as accessible to each man, woman, and child as their next breath. And it could lead from that moment to unimagined possibilities.

Drawing upon the wisdom of Patanjali, my father's teaching was based upon a few unshakable premises.

He respected, and perhaps even more importantly *accepted*, that each individual is absolutely unique. Every man and woman is unlike any who ever lived and died in the past, or who will ever be born in the future. Moreover, each individual not only has a unique identity by birth, family upbringing, and culture, but also changes uniquely at every moment of his existence. Given this unique, mutating existence, however, Krishnamacharya believed that all individuals possessed an identical, inborn capacity—an inner temple, so to speak. There, the self might attain a harmonious immersion in the Absolute.

What is self-harmony?

It is the union of body, mind, and spirit.

How is it achieved?

Practically speaking, it begins with physical health.

Krishnamacharya knew full well that no one strives toward perfection or meditates upon God while suffering a migraine headache, an asthmatic attack, or a wrenching pain of back muscles or bowels. Yet, his view of physical health was that it was more than a feeling of well-being. Health originated in something greater, inexplicable by even the most advanced biomedical sciences. This might be called the power of healing, and this was very much a question of relationship—whether with a physician, with a teacher, or, above all in my father's belief, with God. In such relationships we are brought to "wholeness." Interestingly, in the English language the words "whole" and "heal" derive from the same Teutonic roots—another hint from the past.

In my father's teaching, there is no division between "mind" and "body." Healing lies in the mind, and the Yoga of Patanjali is very much a science of the mind. As the mind draws nearer to Truth, the spirit inevitably manifests. Krishnamacharya once summed it up it in a poem:

Where is the conflict when the Truth is known,
Where is the disease when the mind is clear,
Where is death when the breath is controlled,
Therefore, surrender to Yoga.

"Therefore, surrender to Yoga. . . ." an excellent phrase, I think, at which to pause and engage the reader more directly.

I've devoted more than thirty years to teaching Yoga, including many lecture trips to Europe and North America, as well as other parts of Asia. I'm well aware of the range of associations and cautions awakened by ideas such as "the key to healing lies in the mind" and the notion of "surrender." Among students and audiences are those who know nothing whatsoever about Yoga and those who are Masters, just as attitudes range across a spectrum from unblinking skepticism to unthinking acceptance. I may be particularly sympathetic to the skeptics, because I received a Western, scientific training as an engineer, and I've often been among their numbers.

No one ever used words more carefully than my father, and no one, perhaps for many centuries, ever breathed such freshness into timeworn meanings. As we shall discover, the idea that the key to healing lies in the mind certainly does not mean that Yoga cures all ailments. You prevent tetanus by getting a tetanus vaccination, and treat serious infections with antibiotics. Yoga works with, not in place of, the great achievements of medical science. And a word such as "surrender" also has a different meaning than may be conventionally understood. For Krishnamacharya, "surrender to Yoga" meant directing all one's will toward achieving independence, an autonomy of mind and spirit.

My father's teaching first and foremost was based on the truth that each student must be taught according to his or her individual capacity at any given time. Each progresses in different ways, at different rhythms. And each step is to be experienced for what the *Bhagavad Gita* shows it to be: an episode in the greatest of all adventures, the eternal quest to discover and fulfill individual destiny.

Each person will have a different starting point, but the fulfilling experience of the Yoga taught by Krishnamacharya will utilize five elements.

The first, and the usual beginning, involves *asana,* a Sanskrit term for the physical postures of Yoga. The second element is *pranayama,* consciously controlled breathing techniques. The third element is chanting, partly for its healing effect on mind and body, and partly because it brings us spiritually into contact with something ancient and sacred. Meditation is the fourth element, a means of opening our awareness both inward and outward beyond our usual mental limits. And the fifth element is ritual, so instinctive and universal a human act—and so widely misunderstood.

I attended some years ago a meeting of Yoga teachers and students who were attempting to form an association similar to others that have helped foster the practice of Yoga. The very mention of the word "ritual," however, caused an immediate—and, as it turned out, terminal—uproar. A group of participants would have nothing whatsoever to do with any organization in which the concept of "ritual" was even considered. I gather they felt it meant the introduction of a dogmatic element, which could not be further from the intent of Yoga. The association was thus aborted largely due to the misconceptions surrounding a single word.

Others are wary of practices such as chanting and meditation. In this connection, one of the most frequently asked questions is: Doesn't Yoga always lead to Hinduism? The answer: Emphatically not—unless you are a Hindu and wish to draw closer to your religion. Yoga leads to the threshold of the Absolute, which may then be experienced according to each individual's need or destiny, whether sacred or not. In fact, I am often asked to design meditations for devotees of other religions. I usually ask the students to get approval from their own spiritual advisors, because it does seem odd, say, that a Hindu in Chennai creates a meditation for a Catholic who lives in Barcelona.

The life and work of Krishnamacharya were devoted to approaching Yoga and its practices with an open mind and fresh insight. He seemed at times not only to read the ancient texts as if they'd just been written, but also to read behind the words—to deeper meanings. And this is the basis, I believe, of his continuing influence. Consider this example: in 1976, I decided to set up a school of Yoga in Chennai that would bear his name—the Krishnamacharya Yoga Mandiram. *Mandiram* is usually translated as "temple," which certainly was not what we had in mind. My father had taught us another meaning lying deep in the original Sanskrit: "Manda" translated as "darkness," and "ram" representing "fire." And so the school named for him embodied his lifelong quest on behalf of the human spirit: a place where Yoga was "the fire that dispelled darkness."

Relatively few people know my father's name, though many lives are touched by his work. He never sought personal fame, and rejected all attempts to label him as anything more than Professor T. Krishnamacharya. "The moment you say you're a guru, then you are not a guru," he insisted. Similarly, anyone who claimed to be a "Yogi," wasn't.

Krishnamacharya's living influence is due mostly to the teachers who studied with him. Among the foremost are his brother-in-law (my uncle), B.K.S. Iyengar, who founded more than two hundred schools around the world. Also, there was my father's first serious non-Indian student—and one of his earliest female students—Indra Devi. They, along with a few score teachers from all parts of the world who've studied with us in Chennai, continue a tradition of Yoga that stretches back in time before recorded history. And as is right, each of them has adapted and changed the practice of Yoga to meet the contemporary needs of their students.

Against this background of change and adaptation, I've felt the need to bring together what we know of my father's life and work. I'm not referring to the actual practice of Yoga. For that, you must find the right teacher. My intent is that in learning something of the living tradition of Krishnamacharya, the reader will encounter prospects of undreamt-of possibilities, of ever-renewing hope.

Admittedly, there are many difficulties in writing about Krishnamacharya. Not the least of these was his refusal to take any credit whatsoever for his knowledge, his teaching. Except on one rare occasion, which he abruptly brought to an end, he refused to talk about himself for biographical purposes. This was true to his devotion to living the life, as well as teaching the wisdom, of Yoga.

In fact, I have asked myself, "Would he have approved of a book about his life and work?" Equally, I've had to confront the fact that anything written about him will represent such a minute fraction of his experience and his genius. Comfort comes in the thought that he would approve any effort, even if flawed and incomplete, which awakens curiosity about the promise of Yoga. As Lord Krishna reassured Prince Arjuna:

. . . even he who merely yearns for Yoga
goes beyond the words of books.

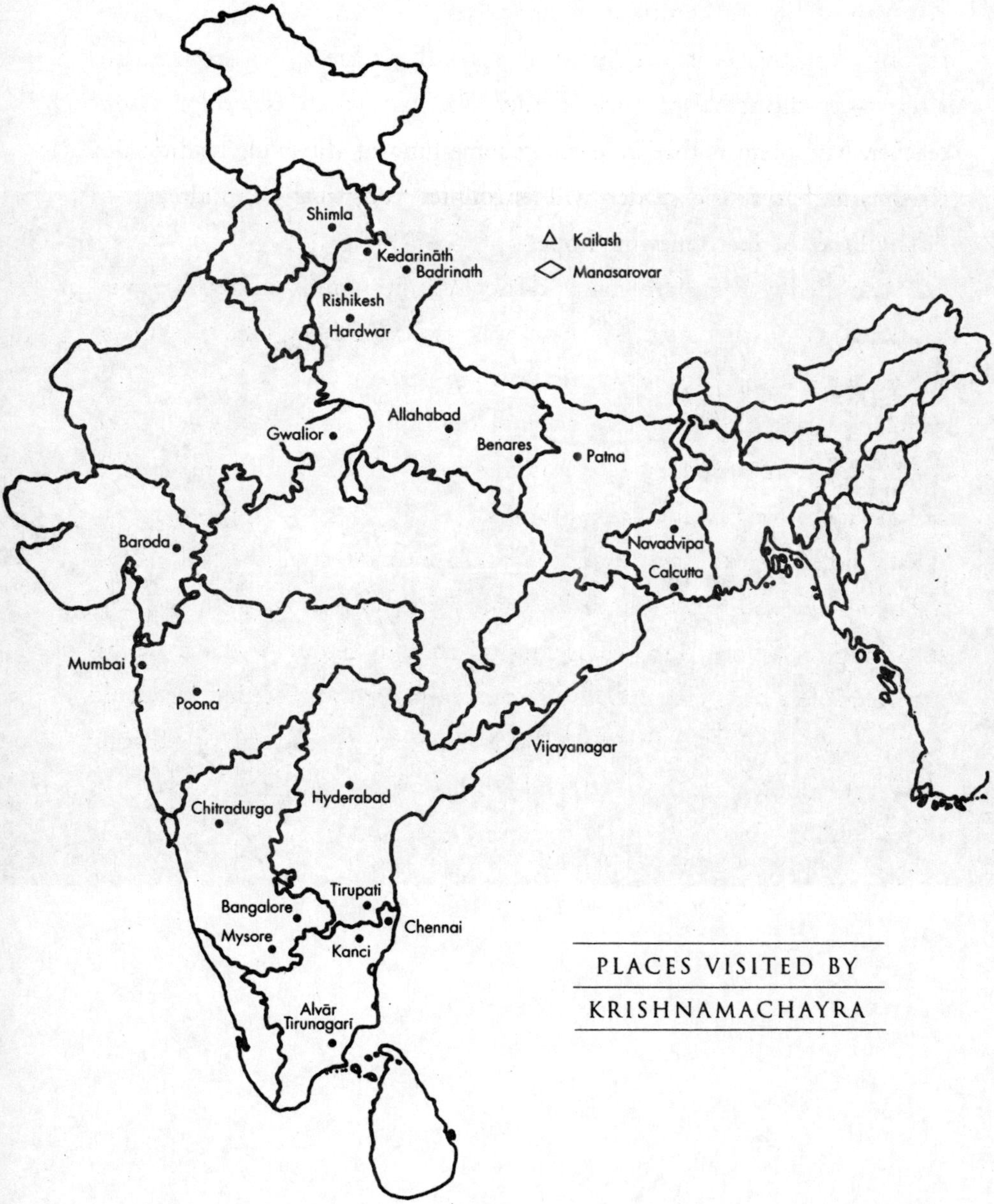

PLACES VISITED BY
KRISHNAMACHAYRA

Mount Kailash, Abode of Lord Shiva, Tibet

CHAPTER TWO

FOOTSTEPS TO YOGA

Knowledge is not only memory.

Every day there must be something new.

In 1935, Paul Brunton, an English journalist inclined toward the occult, published an international best-seller, *A Search in Secret India.* It's about his experiences with some of my country's more remarkable fakirs, occultists, and magicians—as well as with some of our true saints and our "saintly" rogues. Dr. Brunton devoted many pages to a dark-skinned Brahmin he encountered near Chennai, who revealed secrets of Yogic practice. The most closely guarded secret, which Dr. Brunton witnessed and described dramatically, was the Yogi's ability to stop his heartbeat and his breath.

With respect to Dr. Brunton's memory, he might have observed my father doing the same thing, on stage, a few hundred miles away in Mysore. Far from being secretive about it, Krishnamacharya performed this feat on many occasions, often in front of audiences of several hundred to more than a thousand, as part of his demonstrations of the possibilities of Yoga. In fact, his moment of greatest international fame came when a group of European medical experts carefully monitored my father as he stopped his heartbeat, pulse, respiration, and other electrochemical functions associated with life, then, after a few minutes, gradually resumed them. The medical team's report was duly sensationalized in the European and American newspapers of the day. In India this seeming power over life and death attached itself to my father's legend—somewhat more, I suspect, than he might have wished.

I had heard about my father's control over his heartbeat all my life. As a science student, I was frankly skeptical. I would ask him, "Father, is this really possible?" One day in 1965, after I already had been studying with him for a few years, he closed his eyes and told me to feel his pulse. I did, and it began to fade until it disappeared. There was no pulse at wrist or neck, and absolutely no breath. This went on for at least a couple of minutes, and then started up again.

"Father," I said, "I want to learn this."

"I will never teach it to you," he said.

"Father," I argued, "I need to show others."

"No!" he said, very forcefully. "This is not useful to society. This is only an achievement. . . ," and here he used a term that might be translated from Sanskrit as "ego trip."

"I had to do this to convince the public about the power of Yoga. Now, it is done. You don't have to learn this. You must only learn what will be useful to the public, to society."

I tried arguing more. I was very curious. I would have done anything for this experience: What would it be like to bring "life" to a halt, even for a minute or two? But he wouldn't budge. He always felt that whatever we receive must be shared. The worst thing was not to share, but this particular power was not to be shared.

In the thirty years that I studied with my father, he was the most generous of teachers. He would answer any question, teach me whatever I wanted to know. In all that time, the only disappointment was that I never learned to stop the heartbeat.

My father was known as an *acharya,* which usually is translated as "guru" or spiritual teacher. An *acharya* is one who has lived and practiced what he teaches, who is also referred to as "one who has traveled far." That was certainly the case with Krishnamacharya. During our early years of study together, however, I began to realize that I knew very little about his personal history.

The general outlines of Krishnamacharya's life were well known. He had begun the study of Yoga as a very small child. He had acquired immense learning in the universities, and he had studied with a teacher in a Tibetan cave for several years. For more than two decades, he was Yoga teacher and advisor to the Maharaja of Mysore, and he had a great reputation as a healer. But that was about all we knew. He would almost never speak about himself or his past. So, I went to him one day and asked him to give me the story of his life. At first, he refused, but I badgered him.

"Father, people keep coming to me and asking questions about you," I argued. "I don't have any answers." He relented, at least at first. For four days I went to him every afternoon and he dictated events of his early life. On the fourth day, he abruptly stopped and refused to go on. Once again, no arguments of mine could persuade him to change his mind.

One of the profound lessons of Yoga is that all of our actions, whether of thought or of deed, have consequences. I must respect my father's reasons for not continuing to dictate his memoirs. In Yoga, we strive to become one with the object of our concentration. He felt that his personal history was only a trivial distraction. He wished to concentrate upon his studies, his teaching, and, most of all, upon his God, Narayana, the primordial source. On the other hand, his decision had consequences for the rest of us.

Even in his lifetime, a kind of semideification process was beginning to envelop my father. His students and others devoted to him began to look upon him as a saint, as an ever-kindly, gentle, and giving man with uncanny powers, particularly of healing. There was truth in these perceptions. But he was more complex, more human.

Krishnamacharya was gentle and kindly, but he could also be terrifying. He was the most independent person I've ever known—also the most devoted and obedient. While he was a very orthodox Brahmin, he also introduced radical, even revolutionary changes into his religion. Although his faith was unquestionable, he loved intellectual debate, especially about religious matters. Krishnamacharya was a man who would spend hours each day in worship, then delight in taking an opposing religious position and arguing against every detail of his own worship. For example, he could sit and convince you that pure, "agnostic" Buddhism was the only truth, then immediately argue just as persuasively for the complicated ritualistic worship of Vishnu.

Left with the problem of his incomplete biography, we began attempting to sort facts from fables. For example, I've met people who are convinced that Krishnamacharya was the Yogi described by Dr. Brunton, which is not possible. I've met others who claim that in the 1930s he not only stopped his heartbeat and breath—but went right on lecturing and demonstrating Yoga postures while he did so! Again, not possible. More important than sifting fact from such fictions, however, is another lesson from Yoga.

"When we encounter problems," Patanjali advises, "the counsel of someone who has mastered similar problems can be of great help." Such lessons can be learned directly from a living person, or from the study of someone alive or dead. I believe that in my father's life are lessons that can be helpful, comforting, perhaps even inspiring to others.

In his quest for knowledge, Krishnamacharya would allow nothing to stop him. He traveled countless thousands of miles in India, learning the languages and religious precepts of all of our traditions. In later life, for example, he would teach Yoga to Muslims or Sikhs in terms drawn from their own sacred texts. Similarly, he traveled and studied in south India in order to harmonize the teachings of their Yogic traditions with those of the north. Everything he mastered was intended to be brought together, into union—the fundamental Yogic principle that always seeks resolution and growth, never conflict.

Krishnamacharya had the independence, the courage, and the openness to make tremendous changes in himself and in sacred tradition in response to the needs of his times. Yet he also held fast to the essence of eternal truths that humanity must preserve, perhaps for its very survival. The enduring example is that, true to his calling, he lived the life of a Yogi—often in the face of near-overwhelming obstacles.

With this in mind, we have over the years attempted to piece together what little is known about Krishnamacharya's life. There were rare occasions when he would answer questions from students. We've also interviewed family members, students, and friends—some now very old—who knew him during the glorious years in Mysore. And I have my own recollections, and my late mother's, and those of my wife and children. Still, there is precious little information when you consider that Krishnamacharya lived for a century and touched many thousands of lives. It was the same way with his possessions. He owned, and left behind, only a small library, a couple of shawls given to him by holy men, the sandals of his guru, and a few religious objects. My father was a man who lived a long life forcefully and yet very lightly upon the earth.

From all of the resources available to us, I'll attempt to sketch the general biography of Krishnamacharya, in his own words wherever possible.

> I was born in November 1888 in Muchukundapuram in Karnataka State. My father's name was Sri T. Srivinasa Tattacharya, and we belong to Tirumalai family hailing from Tirupathi, the Holy place of the Lord of the Seven Hills. My mother's name

was Shrimati Ranganayakamma. My father was very orthodox and performed all the religious rites systematically. . . . I am the eldest son and had two younger brothers and three sisters. None of them is alive now.

Even these introductory words, dictated in his upstairs bedroom of our house in Chennai when he was eighty-eight years old, contain glimpses of history that stretch back through many lifetimes and thousands of years. In fact, except for the wristwatch, he was dressed in the fashion of any venerable Brahmin of a thousand years ago: a white cotton dhoti, a saronglike garment; the sacred thread draped across his left shoulder; lotus-seed beads around his neck; and the vertical white and yellow marks on his forehead that signify a worshiper of Vishnu. He spoke in a mix of Sanskrit and Tamil, with his eyes closed, and in a voice quieter than normal—a voice I'd never heard from him before.

For the benefit of those unfamiliar with the ancient traditions of India (which will include most modern Indian youths), I will try to act as a guide through the more esoteric features of my father's past. In doing so, I must ask the forbearance of the uninitiated, who may find these explanations too discursive, and also of the serious students of Hinduism and Yoga, who will judge them too simplistic. My apologies, in advance, to both.

For a Hindu, the past is very much a part of our present. Reincarnation, the ongoing cycle of birth-death-rebirth, is for most of us an incontrovertible fact, not a belief. Who we are now is the result of all of our previous actions, accumulated since the beginning of mankind, and with every breath we accumulate even more thoughts and deeds that shape our future. To say the least, this complicates our sense of ancestry.

My father's background might be traced as a kind of triple helix, composed of his genealogical bloodline, the spiritual ancestry, and the Yogic lineage—all intertwined.

His birthplace was a nondescript little village about two hundred kilometers northwest of Mysore. The true ancestral home—both of family and of spirit—was Tirupathi, the dwelling of the "Lord of the Seven Hills," which is about two hundred kilometers north of Chennai. This is one of the holiest places of southern India, with an immense temple devoted to Vishnu that draws millions of worshipers each year. And it was also the refuge of a philosophical-religious school of thought that influenced my father's ability to bring together piety, intellect, and practical common sense.

Although there are countless forms and objects of adoration in Hinduism, most devotees worship God manifested either as Shiva or Vishnu. Shiva's best-known image is that of the dancing god ringed by fire, Shiva Nataraja, whose movements bring forth creation and destruction. He is known, among many characterizations, as the creator of Yoga. His sacred dwelling places include all mountains. Vishnu, for his worshipers, is the supreme god from whom all things emanate. He is the restorer and preserver, who inspires joyous devotion. Vishnu has 1,008 names. As the supreme god, he is called *Narayana*, the sonorous name that occurs frequently in poems, prayers, and hymns.

The gods' worshipers, called respectively Shaivites and Vaishnavites, also recognize many other manifestations. For example, the Lord Krishna of the *Bhagavad Gita* is an incarnation of Vishnu.

The Hindu gods and their worship both originate in and evolve from the Vedas, a vast system of linguistic, ritual, and theological knowledge first codified at least three thousand years ago—but more likely millennia earlier. Along with the religious features of the Vedas, there also developed different philosophies. Perhaps the most influential of these is Vedanta, which recognizes a supreme, eternal consciousness that pervades all of existence. Vedanta emerged as two schools of thought. The first, originated by Shankaracharya, a religious reformer of the eighth or ninth century, was in reaction to the obsessive ritualism that had overtaken Hinduism. Shankaracharya basically stated that all is illusion—only God, or Brahman, has reality. In response to the nihilist excesses generated by this exegetical position, another philosophical genius, Ramanuja, emerged three or four centuries later. In his view, God manifests as Soul, and *everything* is real—all objects, all living beings, all aspects of human mind, and each individual soul. As one writer put it, Ramanuja attempted to give Hindus back their souls, and with them the realities of the incarnations of Vishnu and the struggle of human destinies described in the *Bhagavad Gita.*

Ramanuja's adherents were clustered in the Mysore area until about the middle of the fourteenth century, when Muslim invasions drove them to Tirupathi. Here, their ideas developed and with them a chosen incarnation of Vishnu who came to represent all of their religious beliefs and philosophical attitudes. This was the so-called "horse-necked" god, Hayagriva. There are two opposing legends, both involving thievery, about Hayagriva. In the first, he steals the Vedas; in the other, he is Vishnu incarnate who recovers them after their theft. Ironically, about the time my father was dictating his memoirs a thief broke into my house and stole only one object: my father's household god, a small bronze sculpture of Hayagriva.

Those first scant remarks of my father thus reveal crucial facts about his ancestral and spiritual lineages. He was the descendent of a long line of Vishnu worshipers, and the heir to a great intellectual tradition embodied in the household god Hayagriva.

> My great-grandfather was installed as the head of the Sri Parakala Math, Mysore. He was His Holiness Sri Srinivasa Bramhatanatra Parakali Swami. That was the reason for our family shifting to Mysore.

The Parakala Math was the first great center of Vaishnavite learning in South India, according to its historians. They record that it was established at Tirupathi at the close of the fourteenth century, then relocated to

Mysore four hundred years later. A Math is an amazing institution: like a smaller-scale Vatican, it is a center of religious authority, of disputation, of learning, and of law. It is also a partially corporate enterprise—financed through contributions and earnings as a seminary, a research center, and a publishing house for the works of its saints and greatest scholars. One of the most notable of these was my great-great-grandfather, who was equivalent to the "Pope" of the Parakala Math from 1885 to 1915.

I've mentioned the influence of past lives upon our present. For the man or woman who has led a meritorious life previously, the *Bhagavad Gita* states, the reward is to be born again in the house of the good and the great. But the greatest blessing of all is to be reborn

> *. . . into a family of Yogis, where the wisdom of Yoga shines; but to be born in such a family is a rare event in this world.*

In this connection, my father could trace his lineage back to one of the greatest Yogis of history, Nathamuni, who flourished a thousand years ago. In one of the most mysterious experiences of his life, Krishnamacharya made direct contact with this long-dead ancestor—an event with tremendous implications for Yoga, as I'll describe in the next chapter.

My grandparents were devoted to Yoga, and my father always spoke of them as his first gurus, or spiritual teachers. He later recalled:

> In my opinion, parents are the greatest teachers. I could know this even at the age of five years, that is when I was initiated through the thread ceremony. The presence of the parents is needed in every part of the ceremony.

The thread ceremony, called *upanayanam*, initiates a youth into the rituals and requirements especially of the Brahmin, or "priestly" caste, and so fixes his identity for life. The thread in question is the sacred cord looped across the left shoulder of the initiate, which he seldom removes thereafter.

Probably no aspect of Hindu culture has been described more often and more misleadingly than our so-called caste system. In the popular conception, there are four castes, arranged in a hierarchy beginning with the Brahmins. Next in order are *Kshatriyas,* the warrior and merchant caste; *Vaisyas,* the agriculturalists and householders; and the *Sudras,* or servants. The original division of these functions in society, by divine intention, was to be on the basis of abilities and temperament—not birth. It evolved into an extremely complex system of inherited castes, subcastes, and sub-subcastes handed down from generation to generation. To their credit, the Vedanta schools never had much use for castes. My father in later life rejected the idea altogether. "There are only two castes," he would say: "Men and women." And he gradually came to regard women as the superior, at least in terms of Yogic practice.

> It was my mother who helped me in understanding the significance of Vedic recitation. It was she who could relate to me the things that are needed for each and every ritual.
>
> In education, food also plays a role. When I received my first food from my mother, she not only gave me food but also gave all necessary information about the value of food, what food is good and what food is harmful.
>
> This is how I was first initiated into Yoga by my parents . . . in the daily ritual of taking food. In this context, Yoga means *to join.* Something outside joins in me, whether it is mother's milk or the food we take.

My grandfather, Tirumalai Srinivasa Tattacharya, was a well-known teacher of the Vedas with several resident students and he was my father's first guru. Although the household vernacular was the Telugu language, he began teaching my father to speak and write Sanskrit before the age of five. Their lessons began at two A.M. every morning with Yoga practice and Vedic chanting, as well as instruction in religion and philosophy.

In the last years of his life, my grandfather taught his small son something perhaps even more important. He foresaw that the wealth in my grandmother's family, which consisted of fairly extensive landholdings, would lead to conflicts. Wanting his son to remain untouched by their squabbles, he instilled into my father a deep-rooted, almost obsessive need for independence.

Shortly before his death, my grandfather gave to Krishnamacharya a beautiful volume of the *Ramayana* and said, "This is all you will need." Alongside the *Mahabharata,* the *Ramayana* is the other great epic poem of Hindu literature. It tells the story of Vishnu incarnated as Rama, the perfect man, whose virtues surmounted all temptations and trials. I still have that book.

Because my father was both parent and teacher to me, I can well appreciate his sadness when his own father died. But I was fifty years old when it happened to me; my father was only ten when my grandfather died. At the same time, and with all respect to their memories, I can't escape the feeling that my grandfather's death freed my father for his destiny, his wide-ranging search for knowledge.

It was obvious that Krishnamacharya was a born scholar. When he was twelve, his family moved to Mysore so that he could join the Parakala Math. His aptitude and enthusiasm for logic, grammar, and Hindu scriptures led to lively debates with his teachers and visiting scholars. "That was how I found out there was so much to learn," he later said. He was also restless, constantly asking his teachers for permission to make pilgrimages to holy places and seek out teachers far distant from Mysore. Because of Krishnamacharya's youth, they always refused.

Krishnamacharya's passion for study led him at age eighteen to attend the university at Benares, the holiest city of the Hindus. Founded at least as early as 3000 B.C.E., Benares (which my father always referred to by its more ancient names of either Varanasi or Kasi) is where Hindu pilgrims bathe in the Ganges to cleanse sins. Along with its colleges and the university, there were in my father's time at least fifteen hundred temples in the city. And it is also traditionally understood that if you die in Benares, you go straight to heaven.

At this time, Krishnamacharya's primary aim was the study of Sanskrit, and so he sought out the greatest grammarian of the age, Bramhashri Shivakumar Shastry. According to a mystifying remark in my father's autobiography: "Within one night [this teacher] taught me rare and secret aspects of Sanskrit grammar. But he lost his speech the following day."

What secrets were revealed I do not know. But I do know that my father's mastery of the language, especially in its ancient classic form, was one of his greatest gifts in a lifelong pursuit of wisdom and truth. It was crucial to the many rediscoveries into the nature of Yoga that he brought to light.

By legend, Sanskrit—its letters, sounds, grammar, and its completeness as a language—is the gift of Shiva. Its history is unique among all languages, however, in that so much of it has been preserved intact from its ancient origins. This is probably due to the religious continuity associated with it. Unlike Greek and Latin, for example, it did not undergo the great transformation from a language of "pagans" to that of Christianity. The student of Sanskrit is always in pursuit of its origins, voiced in divine revelations and recorded by divinely inspired sages. Still, it has not remained untouched: no language could that has been used in centuries of theological and philosophical commentary and disputation.

It is impossible to overstate, perhaps even truly to convey, the absolute role of Sanskrit in our religious beliefs. It is suggested by the fact that of the six subjects, or Vedangas, laid down as essential to study the Vedas, four are devoted to its language—pronunciation, meter, grammar, and etymology. (The other two are astronomy, necessary for fixing the dates of sacrifice and ritual, and the ceremonial rules for conducting these rituals.) The Vedas themselves are a vast collection of poetry, hymns, and prose that govern worship and conduct. They also incorporate the Upanishads, or "esoteric doctrine," that contain some of humanity's most profound and most searching explorations of the origins, nature, and purpose of existence. Medicine, music, astrology, and of course Yoga are only a few of many subjects contained in the ancient wisdom, as well as glimpses of magic, sorcery, and other occult arts.

My father was, I believe, one of the last students with even the hope of gaining access to the entirety of this vast collection of knowledge. The libraries, the universities, and most important, the great scholars still existed at the turn of the century to pass along their measures of wisdom to this relentless, enquiring youth. And, as he stated, he was armed with those "rare and secret aspects of Sanskrit grammar" almost from the beginning. How important it was to him was revealed in a remark he made in great old age: "The relationship between the word and its meaning is eternal. It is not a fabrication." This is not the statement of a linguistic scholar in an ivory tower. It is the conviction of a man for whom the word and its meaning revealed the path to undreamt-of physical, mental, and spiritual capacities that might be acquired and shared with others. That was the path upon which he was set as a youth, and his footsteps never wavered. It was also a path upon which he encountered great difficulties as well as helpful guides.

In Benares, Krishnamacharya also studied logic, and after three years returned south to Mysore. From 1909 until 1914, he remained with the Swami of the Parakala Math, from whom he learned Vedanta, and he also studied music and learned to play the *veena*, a long-necked, stringed instrument said to be the original instrument of all music, much as the lyre is associated with the birth of music in Greek mythology.

In 1914, there apparently was another rupture with his family when he abruptly left for Benares again without informing them. Deprived of all financial support, he walked from his lodgings six-and-a-half miles daily to attend classes at Queens College, and survived by begging. This, too, took a ritual form. He later told students that he followed the rules laid down for religious beggars, namely, to approach only seven households and offer each a prayer in return for wheat flour to mix with water for cakes. This constituted his diet for nearly a year.

Fortunately he encountered a sympathetic mentor in the university dean, who invited him to try out for a competitive scholarship, and Krishnamacharya was one of three successful candidates among more than sixty competitors. For the next three years, my father earned a series of teaching certificates, and augmented his income as tutor to the Dean's son.

> I had a very great yearning to learn Yoga. While at Benares, I used to practice *asanas* and *pranayama*, which I had learned from my father. A saint who saw me practicing sent me to the renowned Yoga exponent Sri Babu Bhagavan Das. He permitted me to appear as a private candidate of the Patna University.

In these studies, Krishnamacharya continued in earnest his mastery of the six *darshanas*, the "schools of thought" of Vedic philosophy. He already had delved into Vedanta, which embraces two of these schools, known as *Purva mimamsa* and *Uttara mimamsa*—*mimamsa* meaning "law." Their ultimate aim is to teach the art of reasoning in order to aid in the interpretation of the Vedas both for ritual purposes and also for the conduct of everyday life. It was by the use of these "arts of reasoning" that the previously mentioned doctrines of Shankaracharya and Ramanuja were formulated. Another *darshana*, *Nyaya*, is essentially the study of epistemology, and provides the rules for exploration and, more importantly, for logical argument in support of a theological or philosophical position. *Vaisheshika* is supplementary to the logical school, and historically is important because it advanced the idea that existence is composed of discrete atoms—a theory at least contemporaneous with the atomic school of the Greek philosopher Democritus, and probably earlier. The other two *darshanas* are closely allied, almost inseparable: *Samkhya* and Yoga.

Both *Samkhya* and Yoga are concerned with the philosophy and the method that lead an individual to happiness, to perfection in this life, and to the ultimate liberation of the soul from the cycle of death and rebirth. There are two important distinctions. First, *Samkhya* is primarily a path of contemplation, of detachment, while Yoga is very much a path of action. Second, *Samkhya* is a godless philosophy, atheistic in the truest sense, while Yoga recognizes God in the form of a Supreme Teacher, Ishvara.

Non-Hindus are sometimes dismayed that our religion can accommodate atheistic doctrine. Indeed, in the *Bhagavad Gita*, Lord Krishna, whose ultimate appeal is for the worship of God according to the needs of the worshiper, also invokes the wisdom of *Samkhya* that an individual might be:

> *. . . in peace in pleasure and pain, in gain*
> *and in loss, in victory or in the loss of a battle.*
> *In this peace there is no sin.*

No less perplexing to some, I suppose, might be my father's final comment on these studies: "By the grace of God, I came out successful in *Samkhya*."

Krishnamacharya's interest in Yoga continued to find support among his teachers. They helped him with additional scholarships, and also arranged for his first efforts at teaching *asana* and *pranayama* to their younger relatives. "I was a bit shy at first," my father said, "but could not help it." He taught Yoga to students for the next two years, which only deepened his desire to learn more.

Each vacation, my father undertook pilgrimages to the Himalayas. In 1915, with the permission of his teachers, he decided upon a longer stay. He had heard rumors of a great teacher, Sri Ramamohan Brahmachari, who lived in the mountains. Krishnamacharya set off for Nepal, stopping first to bathe in the holy river Gandak, which is the only place in the world where followers of Vishnu find their talisman, the *salagrama,* a fossilized, circular stone marked by spirals much like a chambered nautilus. Accompanied by two servants, he walked more than two hundred miles in twenty-two days and reached Lake Manasarovar at the foot of Mount Kailash, the eternal abode of Lord Shiva.

More than seventy years later, I was to undertake the same route on a pilgrimage in honor of my father. It was a grueling, arduous trip over some of the most barren, rocky terrain on the earth—and my companions and I traveled in all-terrain vehicles with excellent modern camping equipment, expert guides, and satellite navigational instruments!

Krishnamacharya's narrative continued:

> After searching, I reached the Ramamohan Ashrama [school], which was only a cave. A tall, long-bearded saint stood at the entrance. With deep reverence and respect I prostrated and told my name in Hindi and requested him to take me as his disciple. The saint questioned me about the purpose. I expressed my desire to learn Yoga and the saint sent me inside. When I went in, I saw the saint's wife and three children.
>
> The saint gave me fruits to eat and I, meditating on Lord Narayana, ate them and drank a cup of tea. The two servants were also served tea. After bidding them to remain there, the saint took me to Lake Manasarovar and showed me different places for about an hour and a quarter. It was biting cold, but surprisingly I did not feel it nor did I show any signs of fatigue—perhaps due to the intake of the fruits or it might be due to the grace of the guru. He ordered me not to touch the water [of the lake], lifting up his little finger which had turned blue on account of touching the water. He told me that many who did not know this had become deformed.

My father's servants, who apparently had accompanied him with some hopes of studying with the guru, did not satisfy his expectations and were sent away. For the first eight days, the guru taught my father only the first precept of *pranayama* and he lived only on fruit. After that, my father entered a period of study with this extraordinary teacher that would last for more than seven years.

What were the studies in the cave? I know that they embraced all of the philosophy and mental science of Yoga; its use in diagnosing and treating the ill; and the practice and perfection of *asana* and *pranayama.* From Sri Ramamohan my father not only learned Patanjali's *Yoga Sutras* by heart, but also learned to chant them with an exactness of pronunciation, tone, and inflection that echoed as nearly as possible their first utterance thousands of years earlier. And it was no doubt within that cave that my father gained uncanny powers, of which stopping heartbeat and breath were only a part. No one will ever know the true extent of the knowledge Sri Ramamohan imparted. I can only hint at an example.

My father once told me that his guru knew about seven thousand *asanas.* Of these, my father mastered about three thousand. After more than thirty years of study with Krishnamacharya, I know approximately five hundred or so. My most serious students at the Mandiram will usually teach, perhaps, fifty or sixty postures to their more *advanced* students. And yet, with less than one percent, so to speak, of what the guru at Manasarovar knew, we witness thousands of individuals developing through Yoga ever greater health, mental clarity, and spiritual capacity.

Still, isn't it haunting to think of the wisdom once possessed and taught in the Tibetan cave of Shiva's sacred mountain?

By tradition, a student helps to maintain the guru and his family while studying, but the payment for his lessons is not due until they are completed. The student never knows what payment will be demanded. There is a charming story in the *Ramayana* about a Brahmin priest who approached an ancestor of Lord Rama, King Raghu, in dire straits. The Brahmin had been taught sacred scriptures by the greatest teacher of the age. When the student had asked what payment was due, the guru asked only for faithful loyalty and love. But the Brahmin had persisted in asking for a greater price until the teacher lost patience. "The sciences I have taught thee can scarce be obtained for fourteen millions of golden coins!" cried the teacher. "Bring me that sum!"

Although wishing to help the distraught Brahmin pay what was due, King Raghu had just given all of his wealth to the poor. Nevertheless, he was determined that no holy supplicant be turned away. King Raghu decided to wrest the immense sum needed from Kubera, the Lord of Wealth, by force if necessary. And Kubera, fearing the king's power, responded before being asked by sending a shower of gold that filled all the palace and courtyard to overflowing. There was far more treasure than needed, but the king persuaded the Brahmin to take all of it, and so pay the price of his lessons. The holy man in turn offered a blessing upon the heirless Raghu, for a son who would be as brilliant, noble, and virtuous as the father—that son would be the grandfather of Lord Rama.

Failure to pay the guru what is asked is more than an obligation unmet, a debt incurred. The teachings are part of a holy chain of knowledge stretching back from guru to guru to the very source of wisdom—in the case of Yoga, to Lord Shiva himself. Payments asked are intrinsic to this lineage of gurus, called the *parampara,* and anyone who will not or cannot comply is, in effect, committing the most serious of blasphemies. It is not, however, fear that makes the student comply, but the "faithful loyalty and love" asked by the Brahmin's teacher.

When the time came for Krishnamacharya to leave his guru, the payment demanded set his course for life. Sri Ramamohan Brahmachari said: "Take a wife, raise children, and be a teacher of Yoga."

In a rare admission, my father said the years immediately following his departure from Tibet were "very exacting and difficult." In retrospect, it would seem they were nearly impossible years of study, concentration, and industry. Prior to his studies in Tibet, Krishnamacharya had received the equivalent of two Ph.D.'s. In the two years following his departure, and while teaching Yoga, he completed the equivalent of five more from universities in Allahabad, Calcutta, Patna, and Baroda. These, with those already obtained in Yoga and *Samkhya,* meant that he now possessed an unprecedented mastery of all the *darshanas.* At least one of his dissertations was immediately incorporated into a university curriculum. On another occasion, his examiners abruptly ended a four-day interrogation needed for a degree on the first day, and simply granted him the diploma. And lest anyone should think that these were efforts conducted in any tranquil fields of academia, I should add that the higher realms of Indian scholarship in those days were—at times in the literal sense—murderously competitive.

Scholars were then, as is the case in all times and all places, vying for positions of respected status and financial security. The well-written treatise played some part, but far more important was the intellectual's ability to argue a position forcefully, to win a debate that might go on for hours. Flawless exposition, rhetoric, and logic were involved; so, too, was the ability to invoke instantly, from memory, exact references to scripture, commentary, and other sources. In a very real sense, to the victor went all the spoils. My father cites one example:

> In the palace of the Maharaja of Baroda, whoever wanted to have religious discussions and arguments had to ring the bell tied at the palace gate. The Maharaja would invite them to the royal court and would personally honor them with shawls, dhotis, and other presents. Those who won in the debate and discussions would be considered the guru of the Maharaja.

Those who lost, of course, might be out of a job.

On at least one occasion during this period, my father was warned of a plot by rival scholars to poison him. On another, just on the eve of a competitive examination, he received a telegram. Purportedly from his cousin, it read: "Mother expired." It would be imperative for any Brahmin immediately to return home and undertake the necessary funerary rituals, but my father insisted on finishing the requirements. The telegram was a hoax by a competitor (my grandmother lived many years longer), and somehow my father had seen through it, and went on to excel in the examination.

When fundamental religious views were the issue, the stakes in these formal debates were even higher. Not only the skill of the winning disputant prevailed, but also his viewpoint: the losing side had to abandon previous practices and beliefs and follow those of the winner. Thus it was at a college in West Bengal that Krishnamacharya engaged in a "vehement" debate with a renowned logician that, in essence, pitted Vaishnavite against Shaivite. Some of the region's leading scholars were in the audience. Afterward, as my father recounted:

> These gentlemen gave me certificates and expostulated on the religious greatness of my position. They praised me as the one and only student who had learned so much since the inception of the college . . . they all blessed me.

That comment was the last Krishnamacharya ever dictated about his past life. When I went to his room the next afternoon, he refused to continue. I suspect, although I cannot be sure, that it was because he had allowed himself a hint of self-praise. Patanjali warns that even in the most advanced state of Yoga, when clarity and freedom have been obtained, there still remains the "possibility of distraction from this aim [when] disturbing past impressions are likely to surface." Such, for my father, would have been even a moment of self-satisfaction.

There are a few other scraps of information in his memoirs, which amount to slightly more than eleven typewritten, double-spaced pages in translation. Included are references and names too obscure for all but the most specialized of scholars. There are suggestions that the period immediately following his departure from Tibet took their toll on even his near-indomitable constitution. Twice, he mentions suddenly falling unconscious during his travels, including one occasion when he:

> . . . had an illusion that two bright objects were presented before me while performing my morning oblations to the Sun God. One of the objects was small and the other, a big one, which was reddish in color while the smaller one was white. The effects of the brightness might have been the reason for my being unconscious.

My father was no stranger to mystical visions. Whether this was one, and what it meant, I do not know.

Looking back from the vantage point of the present, one thing is certain: all of those rivals and competitors who envied and feared my father had absolutely nothing to worry about. Because of his reputation as a scholar and healer, he had already been offered important positions at different universities and also in the courts of several princely potentates. He was also invited to become Swami of the Parakala Math, the leadership once held by his late great-grandfather. He was to decline this exalted position three times in the course of his life. Krishnamacharya remained obedient to his guru's command. This meant, first of all, that he would be a teacher of Yoga—which then and for many years afterward was about the lowest possible position of status for any Brahmin, and virtually a sentence of poverty.

Krishnamacharya had also pledged to be a householder, to marry and raise children and take part in everyday life. And so in 1925, he married by arrangement my mother, Shrimati Namagiriamma. In their wedding portrait, she stands beside my father looking shy and afraid. And she was. She was uneducated, from a poor family, and just eleven years old—and she had just wed a stern, middle-aged Brahmin famous for his learning and also, in those days, for a formidable temper. Their marriage lasted nearly sixty years, and I believe that she was somewhat afraid of my father until the day she died.

At the outset of their marriage, however, my mother's and father's first challenge was simple survival. My father could then have been a lawyer, a doctor, a university professor, or a professional scholar. But Yoga teachers made no money. My parents had little to eat, and, at one point, Krishnamacharya's only clothing was a loincloth made from a piece of my mother's sari.

Destiny can unfold as romance, however. That is why we Indians are so passionately attached to the traditions and lessons of the *Ramayana,* to the loves and adventures of Lord Rama and his consort, Sita. There was a kind of fairy-tale quality to the next phase of my father's life. Within a couple of years of his marriage, he was suddenly plucked from obscurity and poverty to an honored position in the most glamorous setting in British-ruled India, the court of the Maharaja of Mysore.

Photograph by Pierre Courtejoie

RIGHT TOP:
The Maharaja of Kholapur, a student of Krishnamacharya demonstrating bharadvajasana, *1940*

RIGHT BOTTOM:
Krishnaraja Wodeyar, Maharaja of Mysore, a patron and student of Krishnamacharya

PREVIOUS PAGE:
Sculpture of Patanjali in the Krishnamacharya Yoga Mandiram

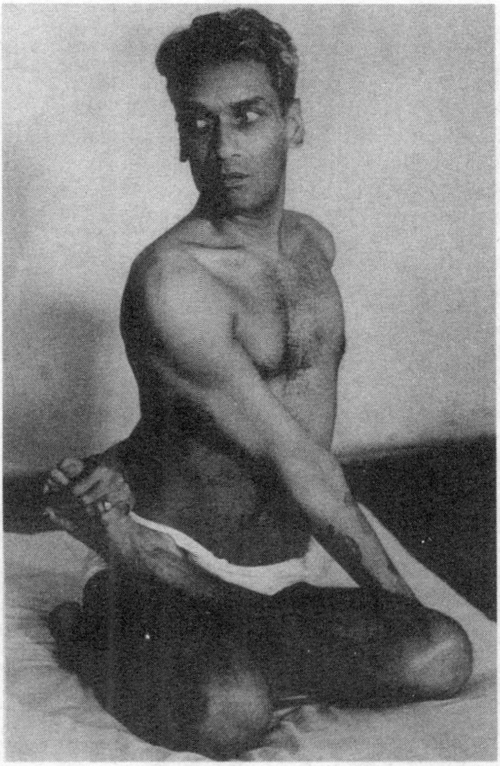

ABOVE:
Mount Kailash, Tibet

RIGHT:
Krishnamacharya and Shrimati Namagiriamma at their wedding, Bangalore, 1925

FOLLOWING PAGES:
Krishnamacharya with his students at the Yogashala in Jaganmohan Palace, Mysore, 1934

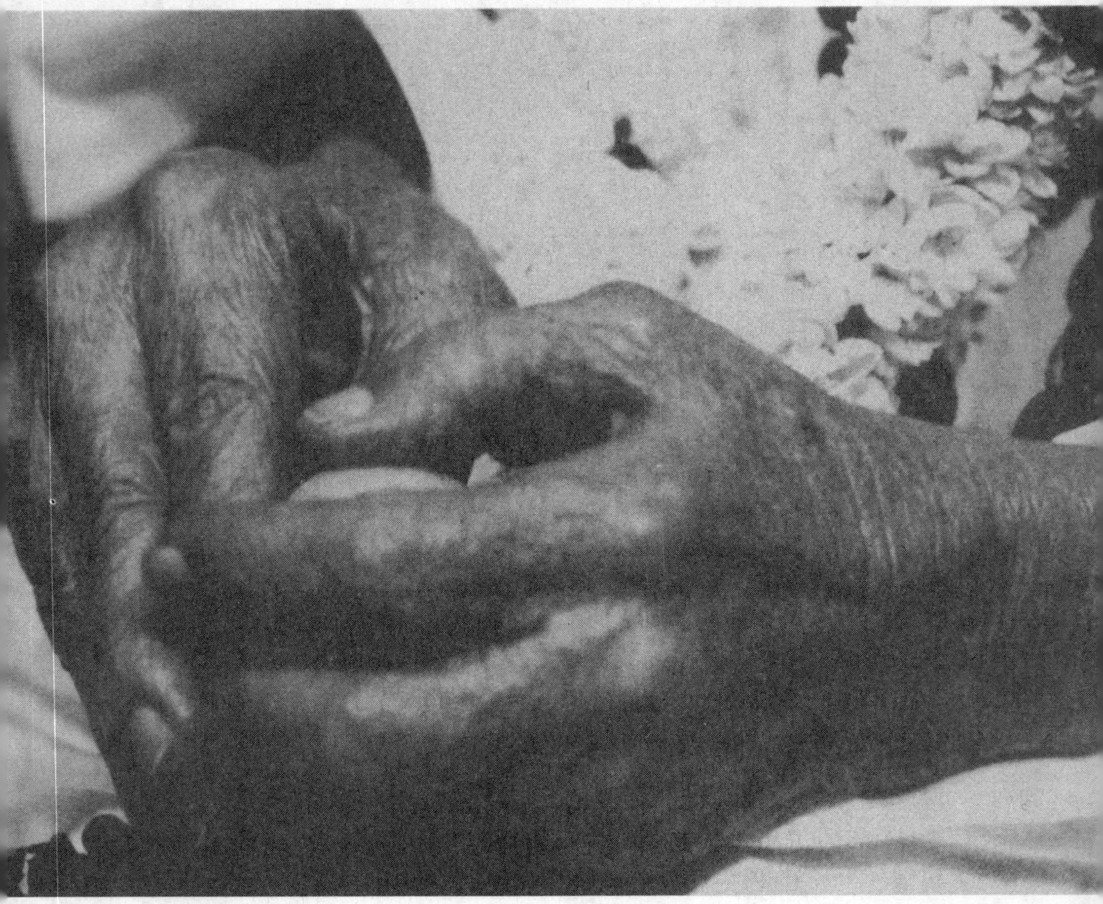

ABOVE:
The healing hands of Krishnamacharya, 1988

RIGHT:
A fragment from Krishnamacharya's handwritten autobiography

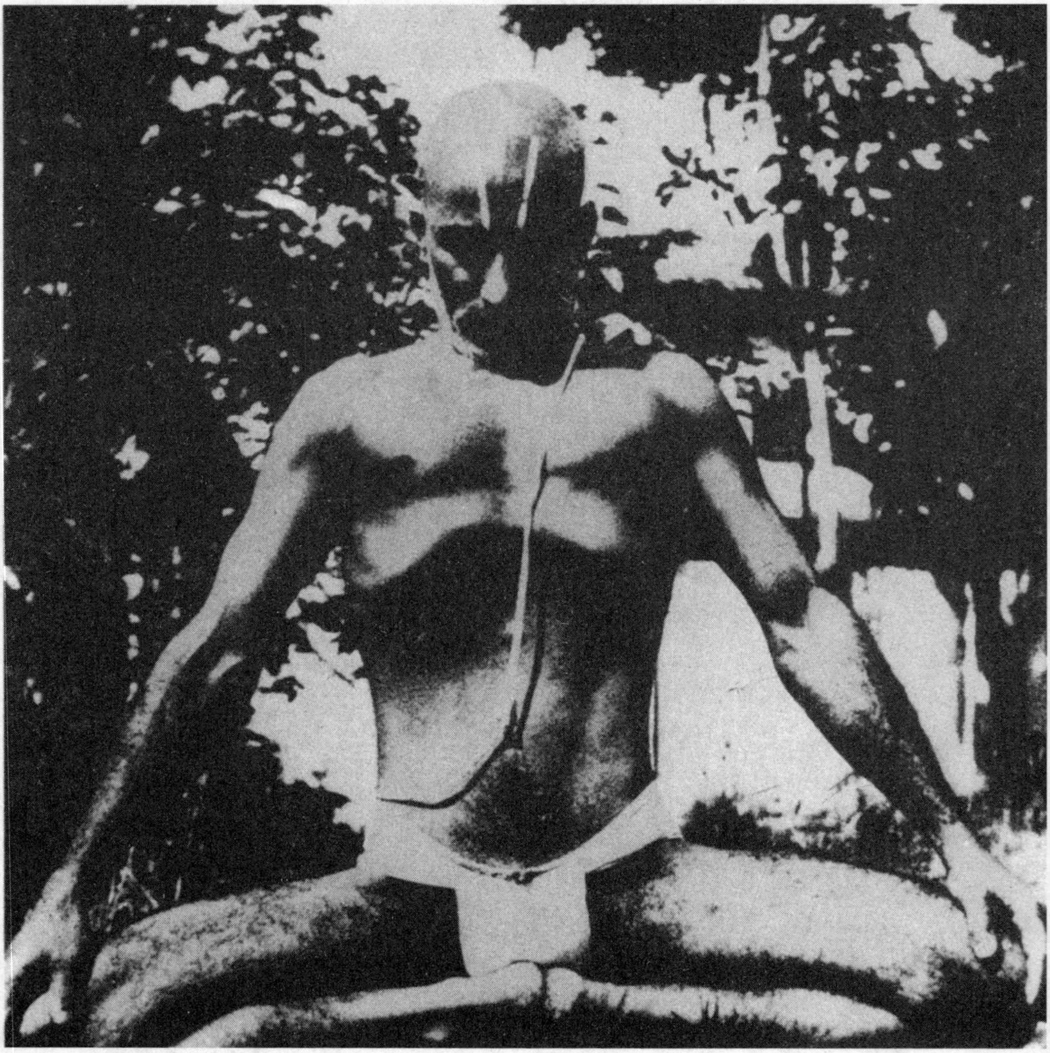

Krishnamacharya in the Yoga Position Mulabandhasana

CHAPTER THREE

THE ANCIENT TEACHINGS

No one is wise by birth, for Wisdom results from one's efforts.

Before pursuing further Krishnamacharya's life story, I believe it would be helpful to acquaint the reader somewhat more with the origins and nature of Yoga, his life's work. He was descended from a pure Yogic lineage: there were specific traditions to which he adhered and into which, both literally and figuratively, he breathed new meaning.

For many centuries, it was believed that Yoga, and all other aspects of advanced Indian culture, arrived with the Aryan invasion, around 1500 B.C. The Aryans were a tall, light-skinned, Sanskrit-speaking people with ancestral branches that had occupied ancient Persia. Aryans alone were credited with the genius necessary to create our country's marvelous heritage of art, architecture, and urban civilization as well as her religious, social, and economic institutions. Obviously, this was offensive to the darker-skinned Indians of the south, where there are also magnificent literary and philosophical traditions evolving from indigenous cultures. But there was little evidence to refute the racial theory of cultural origins until—coincidentally, just about the time my father embarked on his career as a teacher—the discovery of the Indus Valley civilization. Excavations at two great cities, Mohenjo-Daro and Harappa, proved the existence of a highly developed culture at least a thousand years earlier than the Aryan invasion.

Writing about the Indus civilization, John Marshall, the first archaeologist to excavate Mohenjo-Daro, wrote in *Mohenjo-Daro and the Indus Civilization*, 1931:

> Again and again, there is nothing that we know of in prehistoric Egypt or Mesopotamia or anywhere else in Western Asia to compare with the well-built baths in commodious houses of the citizens of Mohenjo-Daro. In those countries money and thought were lavished on the building of magnificent temples for the gods and the palaces and tombs of kings, but the rest of the people seemingly had to content themselves with insignificant dwellings in mud. In the Indus Valley, the picture is reversed and the finest structures are those erected for the convenience of the citizens. . . . the Great Bath at Mohenjo-Daro and its roomy and serviceable houses, with their ubiquitous wells and bathrooms and elaborate systems of drainage, evidence that the ordinary townspeople enjoyed here a degree of comfort and luxury unexampled in other parts of the then civilized world.

Although there are no traces of Indo-European influence, there are in the Indus Valley signs of the beginnings of worship of Shiva and of the Mother Goddess. The origins of Hinduism may therefore be indigenous to India, not an import. The art, too, is unique, especially the seals, which have been found by the thousands. They are small, flat rectangles cut from soapstone and carved with images that are often quite intricate. It was while examining several of these seals with images representing the so-called proto-Shiva that one of our students, the gifted teacher Yan

Dhyansky, had a striking insight. He recognized that the seated Shiva was actually in one of the most demanding Yoga postures, the *mulabandhasana,* which Yan had seen as performed in a photograph of my father.

In *mulabandhasana,* the practitioner begins in a seated position with the soles of the feet touching, toes pointing forward, the knees extended outward. He grasps the feet, each with its corresponding hand, and raises the heels so that the toes touch the ground. The Yogi then places his hands on the ground, using them to raise himself over the feet, reversing them flat on the floor, so that the toes are directed backward, and sits on them. Simultaneously, he greatly contracts the area below the navel—the lower abdomen pressing inward and up.

Even for adepts, this position is not easy because it requires extraordinary flexibility to completely twist and reverse the ankle joints from their normal angle and then rest the body's weight upon them. And it is this complexity and difficulty that makes Yan's argument so compelling. There can be no simple case of coincidental similarity of postures: the Shiva represented on the seals, like the image of my father, depicts Yogic mastery.

The implications are greater than a view of history that somewhat mollifies southern Indians. Yan's thesis not only suggests that Hinduism is native to India. It also helps demonstrate that Yoga is one of the oldest, most revered of all human activities. He also draws another profound conclusion that Mohenjo-Daro and Harappa might well have been communities organized around the principles of Yoga: "absence of political turmoil, absence of external enemies, social stability, high level of economic advancement, and well-being of its citizens."

Our knowledge of Yogic history moves from conjecture to fact when the two great Yoga texts, the *Bhagavad Gita* and the *Yoga Sutras,* were first written down. The former, as part of the *Mahabharata* is credited to the sage Vyasa; conventionally, it is dated in the fifth century B.C.E. Scholars usually place Patanjali's writings about three centuries later. It is important to note that neither Vyasa nor Patanjali is considered "author." They are revered as "assemblers," codifiers of oral traditions that had been in existence for millennia. And while Vyasa's text extols and beckons to Yoga, it is Patanjali who tells us how to achieve its promise.

Little is known about the life of Sri Patanjali. In addition to the great work on Yoga, he is also the creator of definitive texts on Ayurveda, the Indian system of medicine, and on grammar. Thus, he is honored as the sage who freed humanity from "impurities of mind, body, and speech." The mythological images of Patanjali are suggestive. In one form, he is a thousand-headed serpent with four hands, which hold a disk, a conch, a mace, and a sword. He also is depicted as half-man, half-serpent: upon his hood he bears the entire weight of the universe, and he also serves as the bed of Lord Vishnu. It is these two qualities—of irresistible stability and of alert relaxation—that combine for the perfect execution of a Yogic *asana.*

Sanskrit literature takes many forms, such as *shlokas,* executed as metrical couplets; *gadyas,* written in the form of prose; or *puranas,* epic tales rendered in both poetry and prose. But perhaps the most demanding of all literary forms for expressing wisdom is the *sutra.*

A *sutra* is a brief aphorism, seldom a complete sentence. There is no ambiguity in a *sutra.* Yet, its exactness lies in layers and richnesses of meanings that generate endless commentaries and lifelong study and contemplation. During thirty years of study with my father, we carefully went through the *Yoga Sutras* seven times. Each reading was completely different, each progressively more enriching and more profound.

Only a grammarian of inspired genius could have created such a work. Patanjali's *Yoga Sutras* describe the nature and workings of the human mind; the techniques for its mastery; the acquisition of heightened, even superhuman capacities; and the progression toward a state of tranquillity, happiness, and perfected, unlimited comprehension. All of this is accomplished in 195 aphorisms—altogether, fewer than two thousand words. The brevity does not, of course, suggest that the Yoga of Patanjali is easy to accomplish. Quite the opposite.

A perfect example of the form lies in the second *sutra,* the definition of Yoga itself. As rendered in Sanskrit by Patanjali, it reads:

योगश्चित्तवृत्तिनिरोधः ।

This would be transcribed in the Roman alphabet as:

yogashchittavrttinirodhah

Traditionally, the aphorism would be taught and memorized as a chant. Yoga is herein defined in three simple terms: *chitta*—mind; *vrtti*—activity; and *nirodhah*—complete absorption. As I've indicated previously, the English rendering would be:

> *Yoga is the ability to direct the mind exclusively toward an object and sustain that direction without any distractions.*

Patanjali's work is divided into four chapters. According to my father, they represented the sage's teachings to four different disciples, each at a different stage of Yogic development.

The first of these students, Kritanjali, has already advanced in Yoga. He knows its methods and has overcome many obstacles. The first chapter lays out, so to speak, the entire terrain of Yoga—its characteristics, problems that will be encountered and how to deal with them, and the state of mind that results. It is called *Samadhipada,* or "the chapter of *samadhi,*" which means absolute union of the individual's being with the object of contemplation. Although "object" can be a thing, it can also be "anything" that the mind engages, including the furthest reaches of art, scientific knowledge, the cosmos, or, ultimately, God.

Unbounded clarity and limitless intelligence—fulfilled as serenity and purity of action—are the gifts of Yoga, Patanjali tells us in this first chapter. In so doing, he gives us a fascinating glimpse into the genius of our ancestors, whose enquiries into the nature, purpose, and possibilities of human existence still define most of our own efforts. Remember, we are now harking back to those epochal few centuries that gave us Pythagorus, Plato, and Aristotle; the Buddha, Lao-Tse, and Confucius; the still-unfathomed accomplishments of the Maya, and the poetic wisdom of Solomon. Our spiritual and intellectual kinship with the ancients remains immediate and undeniable.

To this order of genius, Patanjali—even in the first chapter of his great work—contributes practical solutions to questions of human existence, to the nature of human perfection. He begins by defining some of the most tenaciously challenging of concepts, such as *mind, faith, God,* and the process itself.

What is mind? Patanjali initially defines it as the activities that constitute it. All our perceptions of mind can only be in terms of five activities, each of which can either be beneficial or the source of problems. As explained by the sage, these five activities are:

Comprehension, which may be based on direct observation of the object, through inference, or by reference to reliable authorities. The mind is able to register an object directly through the senses. When the object is not present, other faculties, such as logic or memory, may enable us to comprehend an object by inference. In other instances, we may rely for comprehension upon written authority, whether a scripture or a scientific text, or upon a trusted individual.

Misapprehension is comprehension taken to be correct until more favorable conditions reveal the actual nature of the object. Patanjali recognizes this as the most frequent activity of the mind. It arises from many sources, including faulty observation or misinterpretation of what is perceived.

Or it may be due to our inability to understand in depth what we see, often as a result of past experiences and conditioning. The error may be recognized later or never at all. A fundamental aim of Yoga practice is to recognize and control the causes of misapprehension.

Imagination is comprehension of an object based only on words and expressions, even though the object is absent. This happens in the absence of any direct perception. The meaning, connotations, or implications of descriptive words may guide imagination toward comprehension—helped even further if the words are used poetically or persuasively. Imagination also arises from or is shaped by dreams, feelings, and emotional states. Past experiences, stored as memory, contribute to this mental activity.

Deep sleep, a regular condition for living beings, occurs when the mind is overcome through heaviness and no other activities are present. There is a necessary time for it. But deep sleep and its heaviness may also result from boredom or exhaustion.

Memory is the mental retention of a *conscious* experience. All conscious experiences leave their impressions on the individual and are stored as memory. The difficulty is that it is not possible to tell if a memory is true, false, incomplete, or imaginary. Within the context of a belief in re-incarnation, it is not even possible to tell if we are dealing with a conscious experience, or memory, from this life!

Each and all of these activities confirm the existence of the mind, Patanjali tells us. They are interrelated and complex, and each—with the possible exception of sleep—should be considered as a matrix or genus of activity rather than as a distinct entity with exclusive and limited characteristics. Each activity can, at different times and under different circumstances, be beneficial or harmful, with immediate or delayed effects.

With this initial blueprint of the mind in place, Patanjali then offers the first, abbreviated guidance about achieving a state of Yoga. It is done through practice and detachment. Practice is basically a process of correct effort, and it must be followed for a long time, without interruption, as a gradual progression. Equally important, it must be conducted in a spirit of enthusiasm, freshness, and optimism that the student will indeed succeed. Here, Patanjali offers another deep insight into human nature that remains unchanged throughout the ages. He recognizes that the pressures of everyday life and the enormous inertia of the mind pull us away from our goal. Yet he also introduces one of the changeless generosities of Yoga: that the very nature of correct practice fuels its own motivation. Distraction and resistance simply fall away, and we gain renewing energy and eagerness to continue. Ever practical, Patanjali also sounds the first warning that we may become so enamored of our newfound skills and clarity that they, in themselves, may tempt and attach us and so impede progress. As we shall see, Patanjali's teaching is imbued with the need for cautionary self-reflection.

Given the vast numbers with whom we share the world—millions in his day, billions in our own—Patanjali observes that there are a few individuals who appear to be born in a state of Yoga. They neither practice nor discipline themselves. But such individuals are rare. They cannot be copied and should not be emulated. In a striking voice that echoes from ancient times to recent scandals concerning "fallen gurus," Patanjali observes that some of these born Yogis may succumb to worldly influences and so lose their superior qualities.

But what of the rest of us? Do we really have a chance of achieving this perfected state of Yoga? Patanjali's answer embraces two additional definitions of a fundamental nature.

> *Through faith, which will give sufficient energy to achieve success against all odds, direction will be maintained. The realization of the goal of Yoga is a matter of time.*

What is faith? We are told that it is the unshakeable conviction that we can arrive at the goal. We must not be lulled by complacency in success or discouraged by failure; it is a matter of working steadily through all distractions.

The more intense the faith and effort, the nearer we draw to the goal. However, Patanjali also recognizes that the depth of faith will vary with different individuals, and indeed at different levels at different times within the same individual. An inborn or acquired faith in God is the greatest help, because "offering regular prayers to God with a feeling of submission to his power surely enables the state of Yoga to be achieved."

And what is God?

> *. . . the Supreme Being whose actions are never based on misapprehension . . . [Who knows] everything there is to be known.*

It is comprehension beyond any human conception or comparison.

> *God is eternal . . . the ultimate teacher* [Ishvara] *. . . the source of Guidance for all teachers: past, present, and future.*

The nature and qualities of God differ from culture to culture and religion to religion. Patanjali emphasizes that it is not our differences, but our attitude of respect, our expression of God without inner conflicts that matters most. We establish this relationship through various means. These include reciting the names of God, prayer, and contemplation—provided they are not mechanical repetitions but profound acts of conscious thought, consideration, and respect. Such acts of faith will enable the student to pursue Yoga undisturbed by interruptions.

On the subject of interruptions, Patanjali lists nine that singly or in combination are familiar to people of all places and eras: illness, mental stagnation, doubts, lack of foresight, fatigue, overindulgence, illusions about one's true state of mind, lack of perseverance, and regression.

Such obstacles encourage distractions. We can tell when they are taking root, according to Patanjali, by such symptoms as mental discomfort, negative thinking, the inability to be at ease in different body postures, and difficulty in controlling one's breath. The sage then touches upon solutions that help us to overcome the problems, including:

- Adopting a more positive attitude toward others;
- Correctly taught techniques of breathing;
- Regular and far-reaching inquiry into the role of the senses;
- Inquiry into the mysteries of life itself;
- Recourse to the counsel of someone who has mastered similar problems;
- Inquiry into our dreams, our sleep.

In sum, Patanjali suggests that we channel our curiosity and our mental powers into areas of fruitful interest as a means of calming the mind. Even the simplest objects of inquiry, such as the first cry of an infant, can help. Or we can elevate the subject matter into the most abstruse realms, for example, a mathematical hypothesis. These are only calming efforts, however, and should not replace the main goal of changing our state of mind from one of distraction to direction. This, the goal of Yoga, has unimaginable consequences. The teacher rounds out his first chapter with tantalizing hints of the possibilities.

For those who master Yoga, nothing is beyond comprehension. "The mind can follow and help understand the simple and the complex, the infinite and the infinitesimal, the perceptible and the imperceptible." This is possible because the mind in its entirety is free for total immersion in the object of inquiry; it is like "a flawless diamond [that] reflects only the features of the object and nothing else."

Yoga is a gradual progression toward pure perception, unlimited in scope. In fact, nothing is beyond the comprehension of the mind except "the very source of perception within us." In a state of Yoga, an "individual begins to truly know himself." What he sees and shares with others is free from error. "His knowledge is no longer based on memory or inference.

It is spontaneous and at both a level and an intensity that is beyond the ordinary." Finally, "the mind reaches a state where it has no impressions of any sort. It is open, clear, simply transparent."

This is the highest state of Yoga, and it cannot be described. It is comprehensible only to those who have attained it.

The second chapter is named *Sadhana,* the "means by which we obtain the previously unobtainable." In Krishnamacharya's teaching, the disciple involved was Baddhanjali. This student's path was blocked by impurities within himself, and the *sutras* help him to understand the obstacles and the first direct actions that will eliminate them. Thus, the practice of Yoga must reduce both physical and mental impurities. It must develop our capacity for self-examination and help us to understand that, in the final analysis, we are not the masters of everything we do.

Patanjali now takes us into a deeper understanding of misapprehension and its misdirection of our actions—together, the source of all problems. In its totality, misapprehension is termed *avidya,* literally "knowledge other than right knowledge."

Avidya is a false state of understanding. We think we are right and act accordingly, then find we are on the wrong track. Or we may indeed be in possession of true understanding, but believe we are wrong—and so misdirect or mistime our actions.

We can see *avidya* expressed in four different ways.

First, there are false values arising from the constant references to "I" and "me" which are always pushing us. "I am the greatest." "I am the most important." "I know that I am right." Essentially, this misapprehension is due to a failure to recognize that mental attitudes and activities change—influenced by moods, habits, and surroundings. Yet we somehow assume that they in themselves are a constant, unchanging source of perception.

Avidya, secondly, is expressed as excessive attachment or desire. When an object satisfies a desire, it provides a moment of happiness. Because of this experience, the possession of objects can become the overriding compulsion of our lives, ultimately leading to terrible unhappiness and the waste of life's greater possibilities.

Unreasonable dislikes are the third aspect of *avidya.* Usually, they result from painful experiences in the past that are connected with particular objects and situations. The dislike persists even after the circumstances that caused the unpleasant experience have changed or disappeared.

The final, unavoidable expression of *avidya* is fear of what is to come. It affects all of humanity, from the wisest to the most ignorant, even up to the approach of death. Patanjali tells us that fear is perhaps the most difficult of all obstacles to overcome.

Having described the obstacles to clear perception, Patanjali immediately places another warning sign in our path. *It is when the obstacles do not seem to be present that it is most important to be on our guard.* Nothing is more fraught with danger than to mistake a temporary state of clarity for a permanent one. We must expect cycles of clarity and confusion, recognizing that falls from clarity may be more disturbing than a state of no clarity at all. When obstacles reappear, it is necessary to advance toward a state of reflection to reduce their impact and prevent them from taking over.

The great concern with *avidya* is its influence over our actions and their consequences. For actions based on misapprehension, Patanjali provides another all-embracing term, *dukha.*

Dukha is the disturbed state of mind that results from undesirable actions and their consequences. It is usually defined in terms of disease, sorrow, misery, anxiety. My father taught that it is best understood as a feeling of restriction—a claustrophobic closing-in that keeps us from experiencing happiness and freedom of action. The manifestations may be physical, such as choking up, a tightness of the chest, restricted breathing or other familiar symptoms. Or it may weigh upon us emotionally—for example, as frustration or impotent rage. Just as we can expect to alternate between periods of clarity and confusion, so each individual experiences moments of this restriction. No sentient being avoids it: *dukha* plagues gods, angels, and mankind alike. Much of the wisdom behind the great religions is designed to remove *dukha.* And because it is so perfectly democratic among gods and men, we need not reproach ourselves for experiencing it. In fact, because *avidya* and *dukha* operate in a vicious cycle, *dukha* can be a helpful guide to recognizing deeper disturbances in our ability to perceive and comprehend.

For example, take the executive who fails to make his point at a business meeting, and then feels thwarted, defeated, and that he has lost something. Or consider the unhappiness we feel when we can't acquire something we feel we must have—a new car, an upgraded computer, the love of another. We see the *avidya* of unreasonable dislikes that create entrapping, unnecessary conflict, divisions among us that emerge, for example, as racism and bigotry. And of course, *avidya* governs the constant state of insecurity and anxiety that afflicts modern life, the worries over money, jobs, status, relationships.

Curiously, *avidya* and *dukha* may afflict our finest efforts. We set out upon a path of self-discovery through Yoga, then become frustrated because we do not progress as quickly as we would wish. Our very attempts to rid ourselves of *dukha* thus generate even more.

So how do we deal with the problem and break out of the vicious cycle? Patanjali responds with an extraordinarily literal insight.

We know that the mind is composed of activities that experience everything through the senses. *Avidya* is like a film that covers the mind, just as *dukha* feels like a straitjacket upon our actions. There is within us, Patanjali teaches, something deeper, purer, and eternal. He calls it the Perceiver, the See-er: in Sanskrit, the *purusha.*

Purusha is an entity that dwells within each of us. It is quite distinct from *what is perceived,* which includes not only external objects conveyed to us through the senses, but also the senses themselves. What is perceived by the *purusha* also includes the body and mind. All that is perceived is subject to change: not the *purusha.* As such, it is our channel to the ultimate, eternal, all-comprehending existence, *Ishvara*—God as the great teacher.

Freedom from the *avidya-dukha* cycle is therefore the result of distinguishing between the eternal Perceiver and the ever-changing, often misapprehended objects of perception. How do we make this distinction?

The mind and all else that is perceived, Patanjali teaches, share three qualities: *heaviness, activity,* and *clarity*. These, too, are qualities shared by gods and mankind alike, and even a moment's reflection reminds us of just how familiar is their experience. *Heaviness*—we feel that dullness of the mind, the sluggish movement of thoughts, which, in extreme forms, we describe as depressed. *Activity*—those moments when the mind just cannot seem to settle down, thoughts dart about erratically, and we talk about being "manic." And *clarity*—those periods when we seem to observe, think, and act with perfect accuracy and efficiency, without waste of effort or peril of unpleasant consequence.

In Sanskrit, these three qualities are known collectively as the *gunas,* and respectively as: *tamas,* the heaviness or lethargy that prevents us from doing what we must; *rajas,* the frenetic activity that, for example, keeps the mind buzzing and awake when we need rest; and *sattva,* when the mind is truly clear and cannot produce *dukha.* Each of their effects upon us varies in intensity and degree, and they affect each other. For instance, what we eat influences our state of mind and this, in turn, influences our attitude toward our bodies and our environment.

The *purusha,* however, is not subject to any of these variations. But it always perceives through the mind. In this sense, the Perceiver deep within is also referred to as the "dweller within the town." What is the nature of this "town?" It consists of the body, the mind, the senses, our culture, customs, even *avidya*—in sum, the "town" consists of everything that makes us whom we construe ourselves to be. Yoga teaches that we are in fact infinitely more.

The task is to achieve a constant ability to distinguish between the Perceiver and all that is perceived. The promise is that this is the path to perfect clarity and freedom. How is this to be accomplished? Through practice and mastery of the eight components of Yoga, which are:

1. YAMA—our attitudes toward our environment;
2. NIYAMA—our attitudes toward ourselves;
3. ASANA—the practice of body exercises;
4. PRANAYAMA—the practice of breathing exercises;
5. PRATYAHARA—the restraint of our senses;
6. DHARANA—the ability to direct our minds;
7. DHYANA—the ability to develop interactions with what we seek to understand;
8. SAMADHI—complete integration with the object to be understood.

Let us recall that in this chapter Patanjali is advising a student blocked by specific obstacles, and that the sage is teaching him how to begin removing impurities of body, mind, and attitudes. For this reason, the chapter concludes with a brief description of the first five components of Yoga—those that we can engage most directly—and their benefits.

YAMA comprises:

- Consideration toward all living things, especially those who are innocent, in difficulty, or worse off than ourselves. Thus, we stimulate friendliness and reduce the anger, dread, and even violent feelings of those around us.
- Right communications through speech, writings, gesture, and actions. This is the ability to communicate with sensitivity, without telling lies, and with reflection. Persons who acquire this refined state of being will not make mistakes in their actions.
- Non-covetousness, or the ability to resist a desire for that which

does not belong to us. Those who do not covet what belongs to others naturally win their trust, and with it their willingness to share freely.

- Moderation in all our actions. At its best, moderation produces the highest individual vitality.
- Nongreediness or the ability to accept only what is appropriate. One who is not greedy is secure. There is time to think deeply, to develop a complete understanding of one's self.

Patanjali recognizes that we cannot begin with these attitudes in their entirety. The obstacles within give way gradually as we identify the reasons we hold contrary viewpoints. For example, the near-universal human impulse upon occasion to act harshly, or encourage or approve of harsh actions, can be contained by reflecting upon their harmful consequences. The most practical situation is when we consider that the violent feelings we *express* toward others may be returned by violence *inflicted upon* ourselves.

NIYAMA comprises:

- Cleanliness of our bodies and our surroundings. Cleanliness is more than hygiene and neatness: it reveals what needs to be constantly maintained and what is eternally cleaned. What decays is the external; what does not is deep within us. In this way we are freed to reflect upon the very deep nature of our individual selves, including the *purusha*.
- Contentment, or the ability to be comfortable with what we have and what we do not have. The happiness that comes from acquiring possessions is invariably temporary. Contentment, simply put, is the key to total happiness.
- Removal of impurities in our physical and mental systems through correct habits of sleep, exercise, nutrition, work, and relaxation. Such activities all point to efficiency and accuracy in our daily lives.

- Study motivated by the necessity to review and evaluate our progress. When developed to the highest degree—a process that continues throughout life until its final moments—proper study brings one close to the higher forces that promote understanding of the most complex. There is no limit to our understanding.
- Reverence to a higher intelligence or the acceptance of our limitations in relation to God, the all-knowing. It is in this reverence that we gain the confidence to direct our minds toward the highest intelligence, toward any object of any complexity.

Yama and *niyama* move the individual towards greater clarity in relation to all things external, and ever deeper into the inner self. Efforts in this direction are constant companions to all other aspects of Yogic practice and the process is gradual.

Far easier to begin with are the next two components that Patanjali deals with: ASANA and PRANAYAMA. His *sutras* dealing with them are necessarily brief because they must be learned directly from a competent, responsible teacher.

As I mentioned earlier, the perfectly executed *asana* has been imagined as the very form of Patanjali, the serpent supporting the universe while providing comfortable rest for Lord Vishnu. The *sutra* states:

> Asana *must have the dual qualities of alertness and relaxation.*

It does not matter whether the posture is as simple as sitting cross-legged on the floor or in what seem to be impossibly contorted positions. There must always be alertness without tension and relaxation without dullness or heaviness. These qualities are achieved by recognizing and observing the reactions of the body and breath to various postures. Once known, these reactions can be controlled step by step. This will help an individual endure and even minimize the external influences on the body such as age, climate, diet, and work. It is the way in which we reduce *avidya* at the level of the body, for the body is an expression of the mind and its misapprehensions.

Through *asana* practices we can also understand how the breath behaves. Breathing patterns are very individual. They can result from our state of mind—for example, the rapid, shallow breaths that can accompany anxiety. They vary as a result of bodily changes, such as the slow, labored breathing after gluttonous feasting. The knowledge of breath gained through *asana* practice is the foundation. Upon it, we begin *pranayama,* defined as:

> *. . . the conscious, deliberate regulation of the breath replacing unconscious patterns of breathing . . . it involves the regulation of the exhalation, the inhalation, and the suspension of breath. The regulation of these three processes is achieved by modulating their length, and maintaining this modulation for a period of time, as well as directing the mind into the process. These components of breathing must be long and subtle.*

There are many combinations, many techniques of *pranayama.* These, too, must be competently taught. What is important is that an entirely different experience of breathing appears in a state of Yoga. "Then," Patanjali tells us, "the breath transcends the level of the consciousness." It is impossible to be more specific in words. Perhaps it is suggestive that, in English, the word "spirit" bears an etymological kinship with the Latin *spirare,* "to breathe."

The results of *pranayama* are forthright. It reduces the obstacles that inhibit clear perception. The mind is prepared for the process of direction toward a chosen goal. At this point, the fifth aspect of Yoga emerges.

PRATYAHARA, the restraint of the senses, occurs when the mind is able to remain in its chosen direction. The senses disregard the different objects around them and faithfully follow the direction of the mind.

Then, the senses are mastered, no longer a cause of distraction. This does not come about through strict discipline: if we consciously refuse to look at something, we simply generate conflict within ourselves. We master the senses through the clearing away of the obstacles to true perception.

Throughout the ages, the third chapter of the *Yoga Sutras, Vibhutipadah,* or the chapter on "special accomplishments" has been perhaps the most challenging and seductive. It is addressed to the disciple Mastakanjali, who has mastered techniques of Yoga that enable him to probe deeply into objects and concepts. Now, the greater capacities of the mind become apparent, and the student is able to master powers, known as *siddhis,* which go far beyond the normal.

Patanjali has led us to this point by describing practices that free the mind from distractions. They are both preparatory and prescriptive—actions based on faith and sustained effort. Although we may recognize familiar references, *vibhutipadah* is essentially descriptive. Abilities emerge as a consequence of our practice rather than being under our direct control, while still requiring the necessary alertness and disciplined continuity. The individual, each in his or her own fashion, is entering a state of Yoga.

In this chapter, the student is also tempted by a kind of Faustian bargain. Like Goethe's fabled scholar, the student of Yoga, too, may find himself presented with unimagined possibilities. Without extreme self-awareness and caution, however, he may lose—not his soul, which is eternal—but his chance for true liberation, transcendent freedom.

Initially, the process described by Patanjali is a continuous, if not always smooth, progression through the final three components of Yoga.

DHARANA is the ability to direct the mind toward a chosen object in spite of many other potential objects within reach. The chosen object may be sensual or conceptual, simple or complex, tangible or beyond touch, in favorable conditions or against all odds. The ability to maintain this direction is not possible if our minds are immersed in distractions or strongly affected by misapprehension—hence, the need for all preparatory Yogic practice.

Once this direction is fixed, the mind establishes a linkage with the object. This is DHYANAM, a state in which mental activities form an uninterrupted flow only in relation to the object. While at first our understanding still is influenced by misapprehension, imagination, and memories, a fresh, deeper understanding occurs.

Dharana and *dhyanam* lead the individual to SAMADHI—an involvement with the object so complete that nothing except its comprehension is evident. It is as if the individual has lost his own identity and achieved complete integration with the object of understanding.

These three processes can be employed with different objects at different times, or they can all be directed for an indefinite period of time on the same object. When they are continuously and exclusively applied to the same object, it is called *samyama.* This leads us to a comprehensive knowledge of the object in all its aspects. It is a gradual process, and the object of our study must be chosen with due appreciation for our unique potentials. Everything is relative. What is easy for one individual may be beyond the scope of another. The genius of a Mozart and an Einstein is not interchangeable but unique to each.

Through sustained discipline, however, each individual can refine and adapt the mind for sustained direction without difficulty. In this way, the mind reaches the highest state of Yoga—it is simply transparent, devoid of any resistance to inquiry and free from past impressions of any sort.

But how can our mind—so accustomed to its previous conditioning and patterns of operating—be changed? Patanjali responds with a truth that, at first glance, seems so simple, but whose deeper implications are boundless: *Everything that we perceive is subject to modification; moreover, everything can be modified in a chosen way.*

His first instance of this truth is the mind itself. It is capable of two distinct tendencies—attention and distraction. At any given moment only one of these states prevails and it influences an individual's behavior, attitudes, and expressions. In a state of attention, our pose is serene, our breathing quiet, and our concentration is completely absorbed in the object, oblivious to the surroundings. Distracted, body and breath are both discomposed. Fixed attention escapes us.

By sustained Yogic practice, Patanjali teaches, we progressively extend periods of sustained attention. And here another reason emerges why we must understand, but not enter into conflict with the source of our interruptions. They, too, are guideposts that aid understanding. The two previously mentioned qualities of mental activity—the heaviness or lethargic action, and the frenetic or chaotic—indicate our past tendencies and how we have responded to them. This provides the basis of self-reflection that helps clear away obstacles. As we progressively reduce the intensity of the difference between attention and distraction, we refine the mind to a point where distractions cease to appear.

Patanjali now takes us into the core process of the relationship between perfect comprehension, *samyama,* and change as it may be influenced by external forces, such as time, or by our own intelligence.

It has been established, he reminds us, that the mind has different states that give rise to different attitudes, possibilities, and behavior patterns in the individual. However, the mind, the senses, and objects perceived by the senses share three basic characteristics: heaviness (*tamas*), frenetic activity (*rajas*), and clarity (*sattva*). Most changes within the mind are possible because these three qualities are in a constant state of flux and permutating combinations. To repeat, these three qualities exist and cause change in all objects of comprehension.

There are familiar examples. Time and shifting patterns of the three characteristics change a fresh flower into a few dry petals. The intelligent influence of the mineralogist converts ore into pure gold; the goldsmith, in turn, changes a nugget into a delicate pendant. This teaches that characteristics apparent in one moment cannot be the whole story of the object. But if all the potential, for instance, of gold is known, then many different products can be produced even though they have quite different properties—including use as an adornment, an element in nuclear fission, or a component of a space satellite. And what is true of such an object is equally true of the mind, body, and senses.

At the heart of this teaching are two fundamental elements of Patanjali's wisdom. First, everything we perceive is fact, not fiction; reality, not illusion. Second, *everything* is subject to change. By influencing the order or sequence of change, characteristics that are of one pattern can be modified to a different pattern. *Samyama* is the capacity that endows us with the necessary comprehension to affect such change. Patanjali devotes the next thirty *sutras* to the possibilities. These, I shall briefly sketch to acquaint the reader in broadest terms with his teachings.

> Samyama *on the process of change, how it can be affected by time and other factors, develops knowledge of the past and future.*

Understanding the process of change to such a degree has its parallels in modern astronomy. If we knew the exact date, astronomers in a modern planetarium could use computers to recreate an image of night skies precisely as they appeared when Patanjali wrote this *sutra.* Or they could image the stars and constellations above a reader a thousand years from now. The sage reminds us that if we achieve absolute absorption in changes that occur in the mind, the senses, and objects, we can anticipate what will happen in a particular situation and what has happened in the past.

Samyama upon the interactions among language, ideas, and objects can lead to the most accurate and effective means of communication—

regardless of linguistic, cultural, and other barriers. All of the great spiritual teachers of history have comprehended this.

Samyama upon one's tendencies and habits can lead to their origins, and with it a deep knowledge of our own past. Applied to the changes that arise in an individual's mind and the consequences of such changes, we develop an acute ability to understand the state of mind of others—though only the symptoms, not the inner causes. Comprehension of the relationship between features of the body and what affects them endows an individual with a kind of invisibility. This is an ability to pass unnoticed through an environment, like a jungle leopard camouflaged by its spots. *Samyama,* exploring the fact that the results of actions may be either immediate or delayed, endows an individual with foresight, even to the point of predicting his own death.

Chosen qualities such as friendliness, compassion, and contentment can be strengthened through *samyama.* It can be used to acquire extraordinary physical strength. By directing the mind to the nature of the life force itself, we obtain the ability to observe fine subtleties and discrimination essential for limitless observation. Possessing such capacities, Patanjali tells us that we can direct the mind toward the sun, the moon, and the North Star to obtain knowledge about the universe. Thus, we find our place in the vastness of the universe and its infinite interrelationships.

Patanjali then describes the affect of *samyama* on different parts of the body where vital forces are located. For example, *samyama* upon the navel gives knowledge about the different organs of the body and their disposition . . . upon the throat provides an understanding of thirst and hunger—and how to control their extreme symptoms . . . upon the chest area provides the means to remain stable and calm even in very stressful situations.

Patanjali then moves into the higher realms of mental activity. *Samyama* on the source of high intelligence in an individual, he tells us, develops supernormal capabilities. Through this, we may receive support and greater visions from the divine forces. Consequently, *anything* can be understood. With each attempt fresh and spontaneous understanding arises. And as we engage *samyama* upon the heart—considered the seat of the mind in our system—we understand those changing qualities of the mind that are distinct from the *purusha,* the Perceiver. Once this is understood, we are able to disconnect the mind from external objects and comprehend the Perceiver itself. At this point, one begins to acquire unimaginable powers of perception.

And it is precisely at this point that Patanjali sounds another severe warning. This is because all of these special faculties acquired through *samyama* may produce an illusion of freedom as opposed to the highest state of Yoga, which is free from error. The remarkable results of *samyama* thus become obstacles in themselves.

With this warning, the sage continues to recount other possibilities. These include the ability to influence others; to overcome sensations of pain; to create inner, healing sensations of heat; to develop extraordinary powers of hearing; to develop a deep understanding of the nature of gravity and weightlessness; and even to probe the minds of others. Understanding the origin of matter in all its forms leads to the mastery of elements, and with it the perfection of mind and body. Our senses now respond as swiftly as the mind, which, in turn, has evolved into a flawless instrument of perception.

Still, these powers do not bring us to the goal of complete freedom—especially if they lead us into temptations such as seeking the admiration of others. Then, one is likely to encounter—perhaps at an even more painful level—all of the unpleasant consequences that arise from all obstacles to Yoga. The student is always directed toward unqualified, unimpeded clarity because this leads to freedom. And freedom, Patanjali teaches, is when the mind has achieved complete identity with the Perceiver.

In the Introduction to his inspired translation of the *Bhagavad Gita,* the late Majorcan scholar Juan Mascaró envisions the poem as a mighty symphony encompassing all the themes of human and divine experience. It builds to a conclusion: ". . . made of melodies of light and fire and darkness, the three Gunas, the three forces of the universe. . . . New harmonies now are heard . . . and the music carries us on from earth to heaven and heaven to earth . . . [to] the Infinite beyond the beginning, the middle and the end of all of our work."

Mascaró's also is a beautiful description of the themes that merge into the final chapter of the *Yoga Sutras*: *Kaivalyapadah,* or "freedom." It is written for the student whose mind is so refined that it has become the servant, not the master of the individual.

There is, I think, a frequent misunderstanding about the teachings of this chapter because *kaivalya* can be more literally translated as "aloofness." This has suggested to some that in an advanced state of Yoga an individual becomes removed from the world, from those around him or her. In my father's teaching—and in Patanjali's intent—nothing could be further from the truth. In fact, a person in a state of Yoga is perhaps more within and of the world than most of us. He or she is not under its influence but is rather the source of selfless influence upon others.

The dialogue between Patanjali and his student (in Krishnamacharya's teaching, the disciple is Purnanjali) is so rarefied in the final chapter that it lies beyond the comprehension of all but their peers, both then and now. There is nothing secretive. These words have been there for all who seek them for more than two thousand years. The semantics are within the grasp of only those who have experienced their full meaning. Yet there are some insights to tease ourselves with, especially concerning the nature of time and change.

Change, Patanjali states, is essentially an adjustment of the basic qualities of all matter. These are the *gunas* that my father defined as clarity, activity, and heaviness, and which Mascaró rendered—in a sense that is perfectly consistent—as "light and fire and darkness . . . the three forces of the Universe."

Change within ourselves and those we influence depends upon both our own state of development and the recipient's. *Avidya* may reappear, and we are all conditioned by memory and latent impressions. Perhaps the strongest of these with adverse effects upon our actions is the irresistible, eternal desire for immortality. Much, if not all, of our previous Yogic practice is meant to help free us from this desire: in essence, from instinctive self-preservation.

In this context, Patanjali stresses that nothing can be annihilated:

> *The substance of what has disappeared as well as what may appear always exists. Whether or not they are evident depends upon the direction of change.*

Change is a continuous process, a sequence of moments in which the characteristics of an object or substance consist in appearance of a particular combination of the three qualities.

At this stage, Patanjali goes even deeper into the nature of mind, the nature of what is perceived, and the *purusha.* It is an exploration of reality and an epistemology of astonishing refinement. It proceeds to a state of clarity in which the individual no longer desires even to know the nature of the Perceiver. And there arises a state of mind complete in clarity concerning all things at all times:

> *. . . all is known, there is nothing to be known.*

It is serenity in action as well as inaction. Yoga has led to a state of pure clarity that remains at the highest level throughout a lifetime: the mind is a faithful servant to the master, the Perceiver.

This brief, even stark synopsis of Patanjali's masterwork conveys only a glimpse of its richness. Each *sutra* is in itself like the proverbial pebble dropped into a pond, causing infinite ripples along the surface and into the depths. Or like a Euclidean theorem, expressed with such simple elegance yet containing myriad implications, both practical and abstract.

Consequently, some of India's greatest minds have taken up the question of inner and expanded meanings of the *sutras* and how to put them into practice. There are literally thousands of commentaries and amplifications, including more than a score of seminal works by such religious geniuses as Shankaracharya, whom I've mentioned previously.

In some commentaries, a student will find extravagant descriptions of the *siddhis,* the powers that can be acquired through Yoga. They include telepathy, levitation, elephantine strength, the ability to be in two places at once, life spans of centuries, etc. I and many others witnessed the undeniable ability of my father to control his own vital functions of heartbeat and breath. Because such powers have long been attributed to *Yogins,* masters of Yoga, they attach to the legends and attract the understandably curious.

The cursory rendering of Patanjali that I have given is based on the teachings of Krishnamacharya. It is the result of his lifelong effort to bring the student to the essence of the *Yoga Sutras,* to the purity of the Yogic process freed from tempting distractions that it can yield. While my father had enormous respect for teachers of the past, he was not simply a receptacle. He explored, experimented, reflected, and willingly altered or discarded anything he felt was distorting, misleading, harmful, or simply wrong. This was particularly true in the case of those texts that supplemented Patanjali by offering practical guidelines.

As it happens, my father was greatly aided in his efforts because in his early youth he rediscovered one of the most important of all texts. This was the *Yoga Rahasya,* or the "essence of Yoga." It had been lost for a thousand years, although mentioned tantalizingly in the literature for centuries. How it came into my father's possession is one of the most mysterious—and, to some, controversial—experiences of his life.

As I've indicated, my father was drawn to Yoga and to its illustrious sages from very early childhood. According to family history, Krishnamacharya was a direct descendent of one of those sages, Nathamuni, who lived more than a thousand years ago. This ancestor, in turn, owed his own revelations to a divinely inspired saint who lived several generations earlier, a reputed divine incarnation named Nammazvar. Their legends are preserved as follows.

By tradition, a baby in the womb is said to be both divine and omniscient—possessing full knowledge of all previous lifetimes. It is only with birth and the first touch of earth that the divine nature is forgotten and the infant falls under the spell of ignorance and the sufferings of mortals. But this was not the case with Nammazvar. At birth, he uttered a sound that protected his divinity and his wisdom. He was unusually quiet, never cried, and never suckled at his mother's breast although he grew and developed as a normal child. Believing him to be a supernatural being, his parents left him beneath a tamarind tree where he remained alone for sixteen years without opening either his eyes or his mouth.

During the thirty-five years of his life, Nammazvar became one of the most influential exponents of Vaishnavism. He created four great works, including one that described his inner search for truth and the various stages of communion with God. And he attained eternal bliss or beatitude, which he embodied in hymns of a thousand verses said to be of divine beauty and power. In the course of time, the hymns were lost.

It was these hymns that inspired Nathamuni to undertake a pilgrimage many years later to the sacred tamarind tree of Nammazvar. Well-versed in the Vedas, Nathamuni was renowned as a musician and singer, arts that he had learned from his mother. A priest, he married and had a grown son by the time he heard a group of pilgrims singing beautiful devotional songs that contained a scant ten verses surviving from the hymns of Nammazvar. Arriving at the tamarind, Nathamuni sat in meditation and recited the devotional songs twelve thousand times. As a result of his piety, he had a vision of Nammazvar. In the vision, Nammazvar revealed to him not only the thousand verses of the hymns he sought but also the entire four thousand verses composed by all twelve of the great saints of Lord Vishnu. From this began a renaissance of the Vaishnavite worship that inspires devotees to the present day.

Nathamuni's accomplishments, according to legend, are varied. He bequeathed Vedanta philosophy to one disciple. With another, he initiated the practice that a married householder could be a guru, or spiritual guide; previously, only ascetics were considered appropriate. To still another, Nathamuni intended to impart his vast knowledge of Yoga. But the disciple was unable to keep the appointment and so this teaching, the *Yoga Rahasya,* was lost to mankind.

The sacred tamarind tree of Nammazvar and Nathamuni is located in the temple of Alvar Tirunagari on the bank of the River Tamramparni deep in southern India. For those familiar with our famous temples, either as visitors or through pictures, Alvar Tirunagari comes as something of a surprise. It has none of the towering architecture nor the proliferation of elaborate granite sculptures of divinities. Rather modest, even chaste, Alvar Tirunagari is a vast, rambling whitewashed structure with comparatively simple reliefs—and not many of them—of gods and goddesses painted in light pastels. It is open and filled with sunlight that alternates with cooling shadows. And the tamarind tree is still there.

The sacred tamarind is so-called because, among other things, its leaves do not close at night as others of its species do. Thus it is said never to sleep but always to be offering prayers to God. The base of this gigantic tree rests upon the earth of a small courtyard set in the temple roof. Directly underneath is a shrine devoted to Nammazvar. This means that the tree has no visible space for roots! It leans against a small surrounding wall in the courtyard, seemingly lifeless, but puts forth green branches laden with delicate yellow flowers that spread over the roof. The tree is said to be more than two thousand years old, and for centuries it has been a site of daily worship. The sacred tamarind is one Indian phenomenon that I am always delighted to describe to skeptics: if they have doubts, all they have to do is go there and see for themselves!

What happened to my father when he visited Alvar Tirunagari is best described in his own words, dictated many years later.

> When I was five years old, my father initiated me into the practice of Yoga. When he indicated that our family originated from Nathamuni, the Yogi who received the teaching from Nammazvar, I decided to visit his birthplace. But my father did not approve of it because we were living far away from Alvar Tirunagari.
>
> When I was ten my father died. I was on my own. Years later, I had a few rupees to make a journey to Tirunelveli [a railway station in a district of the same name containing nine major temples]. From there I walked [twenty miles] to Alvar Tirunagari. I arrived at the gate of the Sathakopa [i.e. Nammazvar] temple, exhausted. There was an old man sitting near the entrance. I asked him where to find Nathamuni. Smilingly, he pointed his fingers and said, "Go to the mango grove; there he will be sitting with his disciples." With great excitement I crossed the river Tamraparni, felt quite tired and collapsed. Suddenly, I found myself in a mango grove in the presence of three sages. I prostrated and requested them to instruct me in the *Yoga Rahasya*. They nodded their heads. The sage seated in the center began reciting the verses. He had such a musical voice.
>
> After a few hours, I woke up and looked around. There was no mango grove, there were no sages, either. I was sitting in front of the entrance to the temple. The old man was still there. He asked me, "Did you receive the instructions on the *Yoga Rahasya*? Go inside and offer your prayers to Nammazvar!"
>
> I entered the temple, went around the tamarind tree, pros-

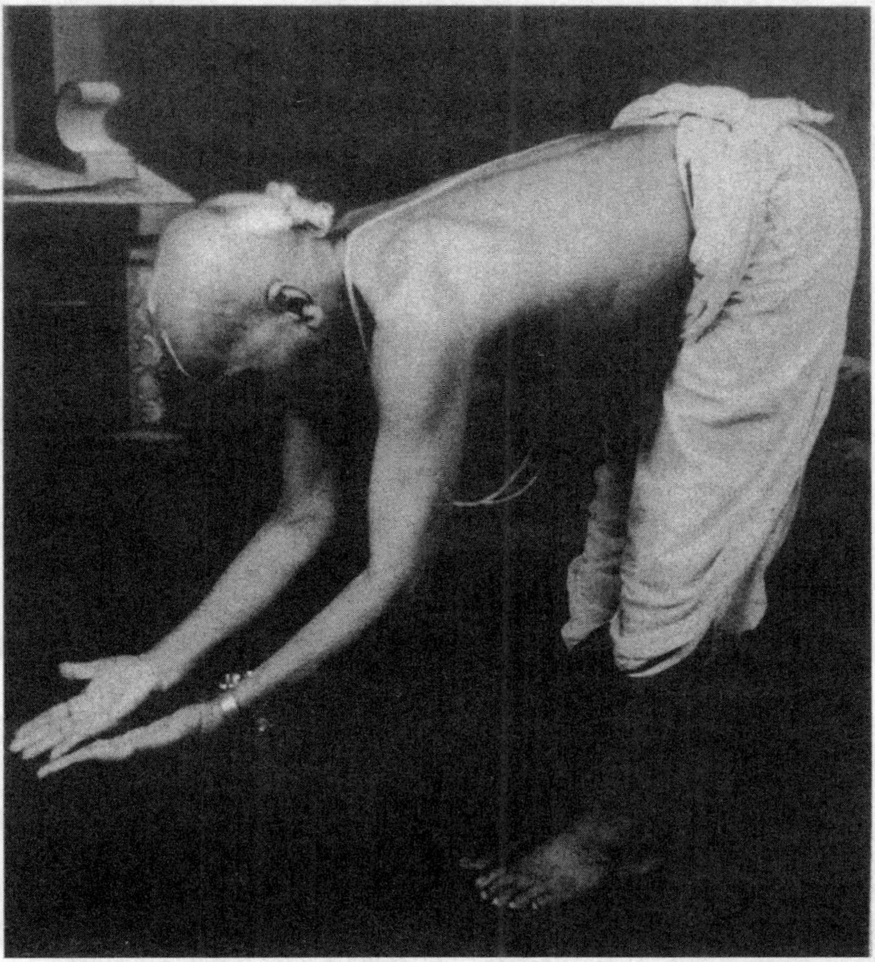

Krishnamacharya prostrating to the sun, Chennai (photo studio), 1966

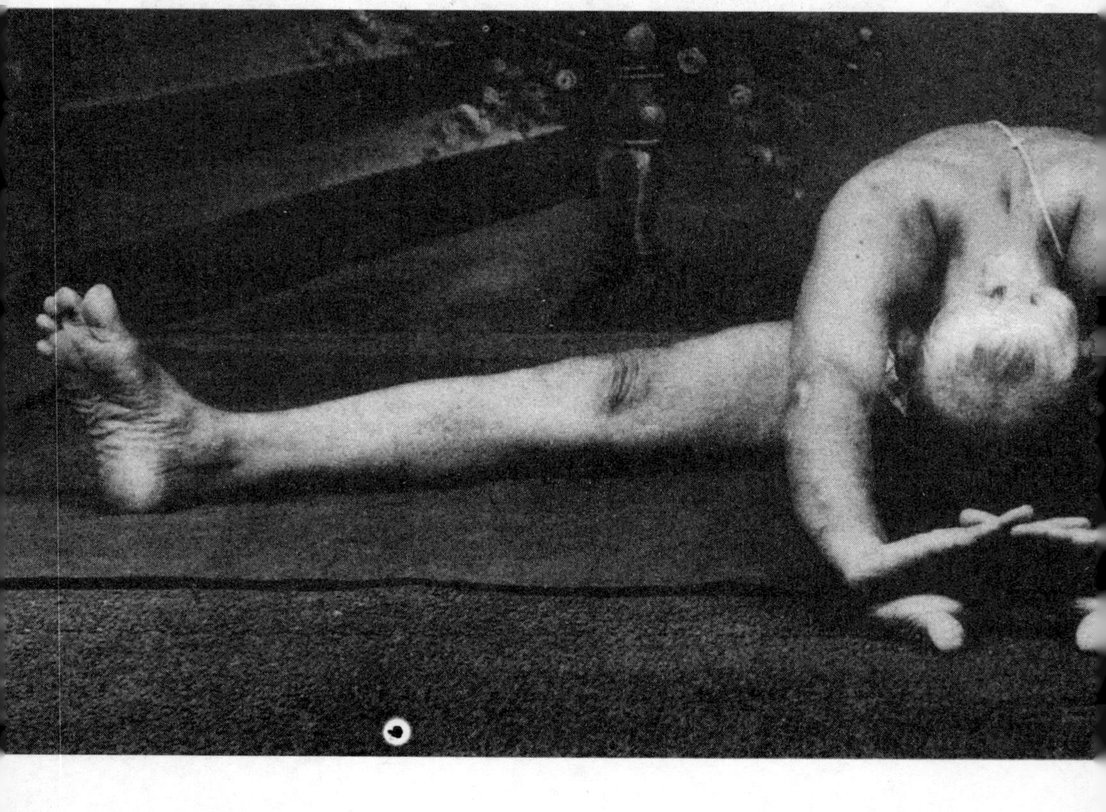

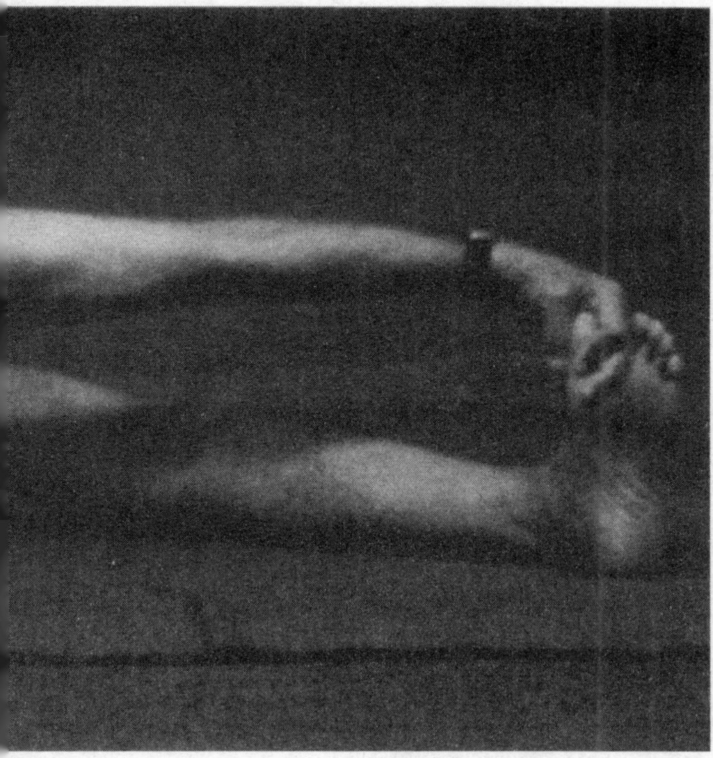

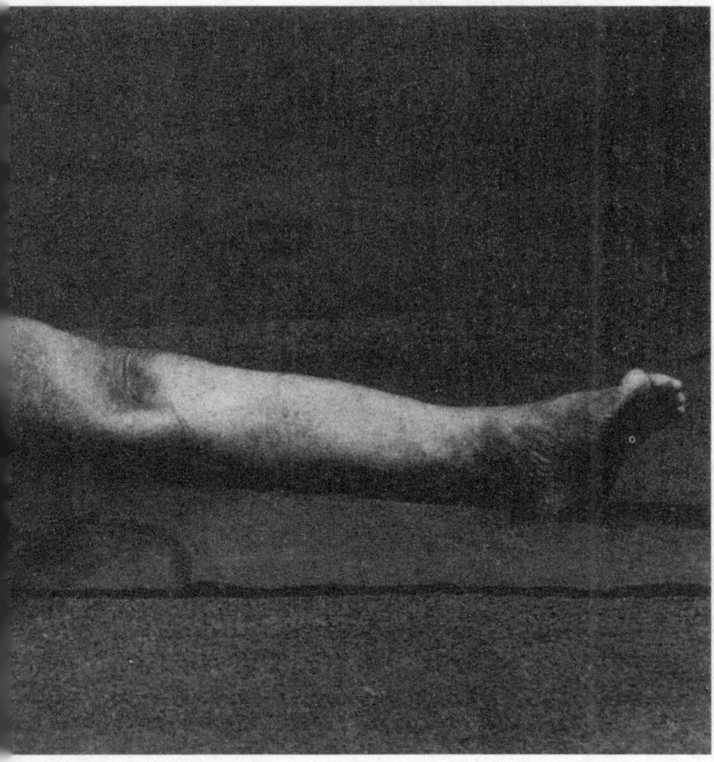

Krishnamacharya doing two variations of upavishta konasana, *Chennai (photo studio),* 1966

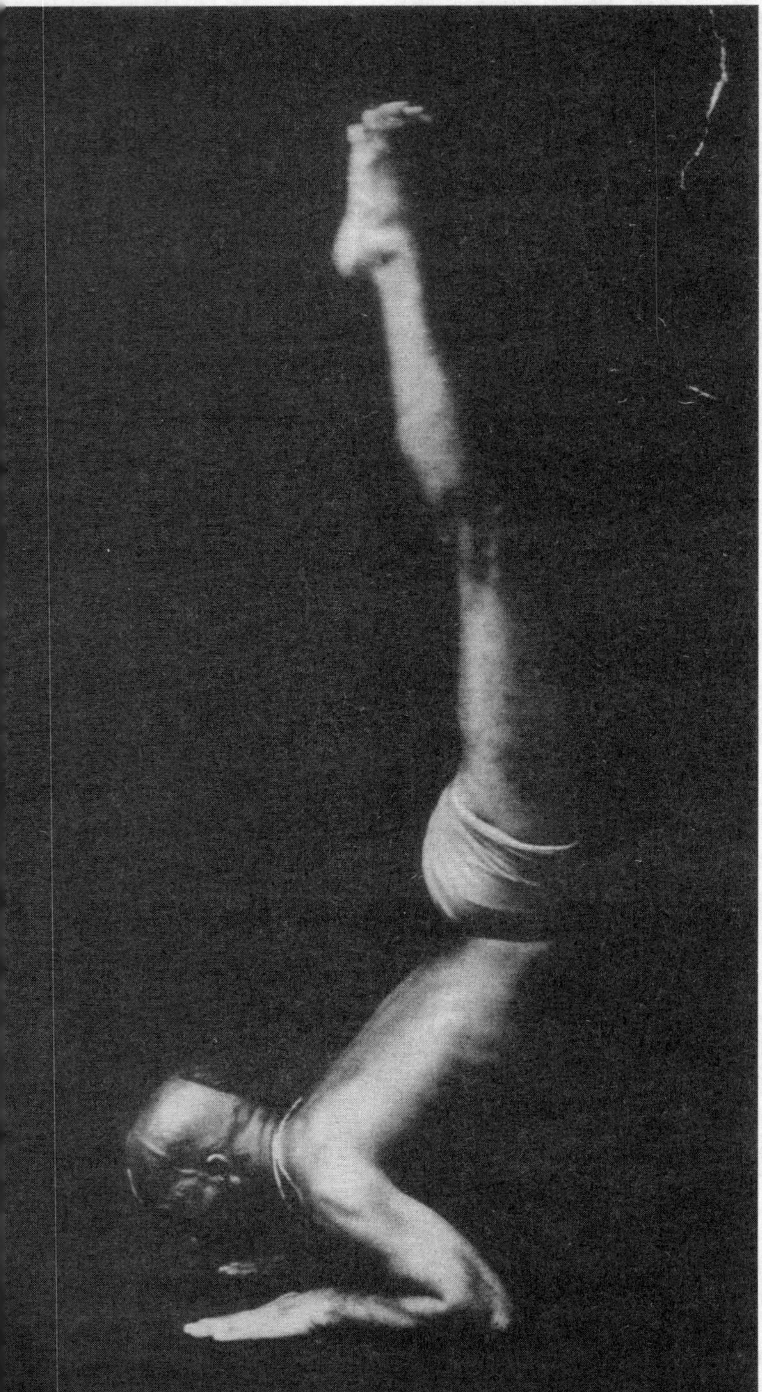

LEFT:
Krishnamacharya in pinchamayurasana, *Mysore, 1933*

RIGHT TOP:
Krishnamacharya in setubandhasana, *Mysore* 1933

RIGHT BOTTOM:
Krishnamacharya in uttita parshva konasana, *Chennai (photo studio),* 1966

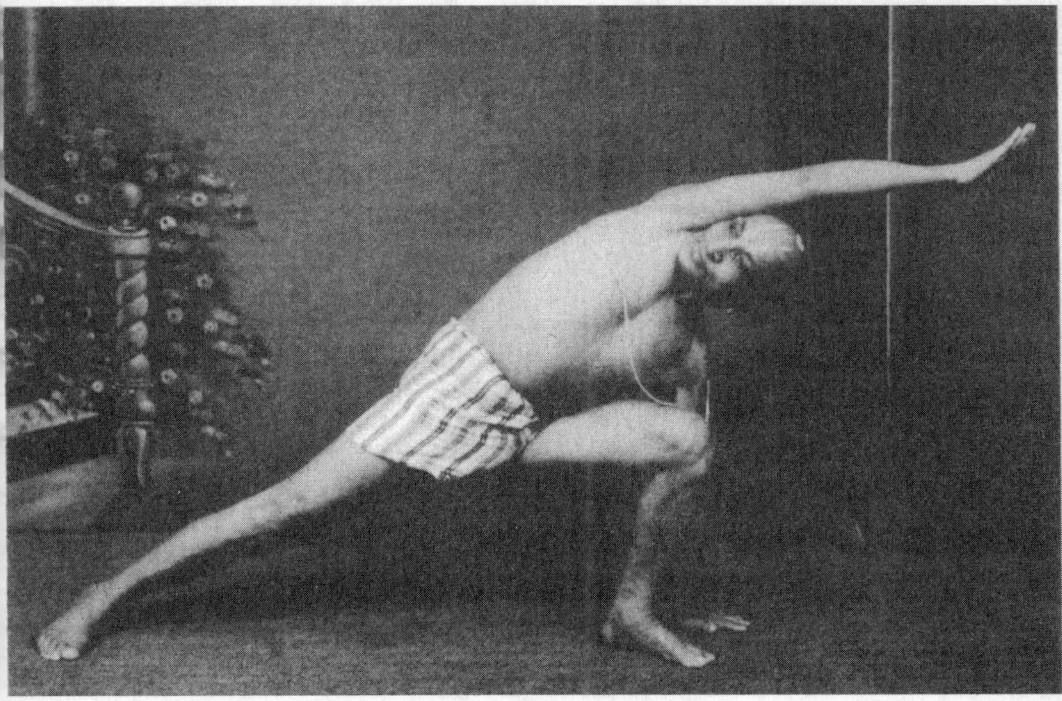

ABOVE:

Sribhashyam, Krishnamacharya's youngest son, in akarana dhanurasana

RIGHT:

Krishnamacharya in padma pinchamayurasana, *1934*

FOLLOWING PAGE:

Krishnamacharya at 73, 1961

trated 108 times, received the *prasadam* [ritual placement of the altar's silver headdress upon the worshiper], and came out of the temple to thank the elderly Brahmin. He was not there. I began to recollect his features. What a coincidence—he looked exactly like the sage who was seated in the center of the grove.

I knew, then, that the elderly Brahmin I had met was none other than Nathamuni himself.

Altogether, the *Yoga Rahasya* consists of twelve chapters. Unlike the *Yoga Sutras* of Patanjali, however, there is no easily comprehensible organization. We possess the text as written down by my father—who had, of course, committed it to memory—in the Sanskrit language using Telugu script, as was his habit. It is an extraordinary text that has had a profound affect upon the teaching of Yoga in this century, although many Yoga teachers in India and abroad are unaware of it.

Nathamuni's knowledge includes detailed descriptions into the nature, diagnosis, and treatment of disease, because: "One may be affluent, be a Monarch, or endowed with a brilliant intellect, but no human being can obtain peace of mind if one is afflicted with disease." No other Yoga text places such emphasis upon the importance of considering the uniqueness of the individual in prescribing practice—including such characteristics as age, sex, body type, and station in life. There is also a great deal of emphasis upon the need for, and the nature of, Yogic practice for pregnant women.

Perhaps the most striking feature of the *Yoga Rahasya* is its innovations. Traditionally, it was taught that *asanas*—bodily exercise—should be followed by *pranayama*. Nathamuni brings the two together, and further incorporates the use of sound and of mantras. He introduces previously unknown techniques of *pranayama*. What I found most surprising is that it is Nathamuni's text that introduced two of the best-known, certainly the most photographed of all Yogic postures: *sirsana* and *sarvangasana*, respectively the "headstand" and "shoulderstand." I and others have searched through countless texts and these vital postures simply do not occur until the *Yoga Rahasya.*

Along with these and other innovations, the *Yoga Rahasya* also incorporates a message to humanity of singular import. It is drawn from the *Vishnu Purana,* or scriptures, and takes us into the very heart of human bondage and liberation.

So often throughout this narrative, I've referred to the promise of Yoga in bringing the individual to freedom, to clarity. But freedom from what? Doesn't a wealthy, vigorous individual with a thriving family feel free from cares that afflict most of mankind? Do not those of surpassing intellect seem to have a clear understanding of the world we live in? Perhaps—momentarily and, in the course of time it will emerge, superficially. The problem of human freedom goes much deeper, and the *Yoga Rahasya* portrays it in the starkest terms.

Endlessly, the ancient text tells us, the cycle begins anew:

> *The child, being born, has his face tainted by excreta,*
> *urine, and the marrow and is tormented . . . with*
> *great trouble he comes out of the womb of his mother.*
> *Fainting intensely, he touches the external air . . .*
> *limbs as though pierced by thorns and cut asunder by*
> *saws, he falls as if a worm from the foul ulcer . . .*
> *he gains a bath, or a drink, or food only according*
> *to the desires of others . . . he lives in an unclean*
> *bed or is bitten by worms or mosquitoes . . . he meets*
> *with the manifold sorrows of birth.*

Amidst a lifetime of learning, labors, loves, and sorrows—the small victories and harsh losses, momentary pleasures and indelible pains—

echo the very birth cries of human consciousness: "Who am I? From where have I come, where am I going? Why this suffering, this darkness, this confusion? What is to be done, to be left undone: what is to be said, and what left unuttered? By what bond am I bound? Is it all by cause . . . or without a cause?"

And with faith or doubt, hope or horror, the cycle draws each man and woman toward the finality of death, the waiting mystery.

The quest for happiness, for tranquillity transits through these fundamental conditions and questions. All of the world's great religions and philosophies provide solace for the journeyer. It is the gift of Yoga to create that union of body, mind, and spirit capable of truly understanding and existing within the serenity offered by eternal truths. Whether it leads to liberation from a karmic cycle of life and death may be a matter of belief. Unquestioned is the possibility of obtaining freedom from the confusion and sorrows of the life we may be certain is at our disposal.

The Maharaja of Mysore, Mysore, 1933

CHAPTER FOUR

THE YOGI AND THE MAHARAJA

I will serve my guru. In this world

I will be a slave to nobody, work under nobody.

Money and status mean nothing to me.

Mysore is one of my country's most beautiful small cities, situated on a rich, fertile elevation that benefits from both the southwest and northeast monsoons. It is where English colonial rulers once fashioned their idea of a perfectly governed Indian principality. If India was, as they used to say, the jewel in Britain's imperial crown, Mysore was the sparkle.

It was a city of broad avenues, arching shade trees, and many palaces—most notably the great palace of the maharaja. On its vast parade grounds files of elephants and smartly dressed cavalry formed processions for visiting dignitaries. The palace's gilt domes reflected brilliantly against the sky, and its enormous, massively pillared reception rooms were scenes of fabulous pomp. The palace was everything a foreigner might expect of a maharaja. No one seemed to mind much that it had been designed by an English architect to replace a rather humbler palace that had burned to the ground. The king's palace was almost brand new in the 1920s, and the dynasty that ruled from it was of recent vintage, too.

The British presence in Mysore was different from that in other parts of India, and even less subtle. Their first contacts with my country began in the early seventeenth century with the arrival of trading expeditions on behalf of the East India Company. For the next century and a half, the expansion of British power was primarily aimed at protecting the company's economic interests and in checking, then eliminating, French influence. In the latter half of the eighteenth century, however, the British encountered their most formidable opponent, Hyder Ali, the Sultan of Mysore.

Hyder was a brilliant military strategist who usurped the throne, acquired European artillery and trained gunmen, and launched a campaign for the independence of southern India. His forces drove the British and their native allies back to the gates of Chennai and almost into the Sea of Bengal. Hyder Ali died in 1782. Although subsequent warfare shifted the balance of power back and forth, it was not until 1799, when his son and successor, Tipoo Ali, was killed in battle that British forces prevailed.

Coincidentally, it was two Englishmen famous in Western history who played decisive roles in the struggle and its aftermath. Tipoo Ali was defeated by Lord Cornwallis, fresh from his surrender at Yorktown, Virginia, which guaranteed the independence of the American colonies. He was more successful in India. And it was a young Arthur Wellesley, the future Duke of Wellington and the hero of Waterloo, who determined the future Maharajas of Mysore.

Wellesley, whose brother was then governor-general, rejected claims to the throne by heirs of Hyder and Tipoo. Instead, he chose a descendent of the previous Hindu rulers. Coming of age in 1811, Wellesley's Maharaja plunged the wealthy province heavily into debt and drove his subjects to near rebellion. The British responded by seizing direct control over Mysore State—in contrast to "indirect rule" through native princes common elsewhere in India. Sixty years passed before another member of the ruling house was established as Maharaja: a young man carefully educated by the British, who reigned under very limited conditions. It was his son, Krishnaraja Wodejar, who occupied the throne when my father returned to Mysore in 1924.

Even Indian historians credit the Mysore government with good administration. Ancient irrigation systems had been expanded, and farms and coffee and tea plantations flourished. A huge hydroelectric dam had been built, as well as excellent rail systems. The rich Kolar goldfields were developed, and Mysore silks, sandalwood, and ivory were prized throughout the world. None of this prosperity, of course, touched my father. At one point, in order to support his family, he took a job as supervisor on a coffee plantation. I still find it difficult to imagine him in khaki shorts, counting heads and keeping track of the workers. Only very slowly did he manage to start attracting a few Yoga students.

Things took a turn for the better because, despite the wealth and glamour of Mysore, within the palace all was far from well. The Maharaja was a very sick man. He suffered from a host of ailments, including diabetes and infertility, and neither the best European doctors nor the most celebrated local healers were able to help him. While attending his mother's sixtieth birthday celebrations in Kasi, the Maharaja heard about Krishnamacharya's learning and skill as a Yoga therapist. Subsequently, he invited my father to an audience at the palace in Mysore.

Krishnaraja Wodejar was a highly cultivated man, and he and my father immediately took to one another. My father talked to him about Yoga, gave a demonstration, and even composed a beautiful poem in Sanskrit on the spot. The Maharaja was so impressed that he engaged Krishnamacharya to teach him and his family. He went further, giving my father a wing of Jaganmohan, a nearby palace, to establish a *Yogashala,* or school of Yoga, and provided him with a decent income. From the beginning, however, it was understood that Krishnamacharya would be no ordinary courtier. He was too independent.

That independence showed early in my father's choice of a house. It was a comfortable dwelling about five kilometers from the palace, somewhat smaller than the nearby homes of government officials. Our house had an evil reputation. A man had hanged himself there, and everyone told my father that it was haunted. "What have ghosts to do with me?" Krishnamacharya demanded. He performed the necessary rituals, and my parents moved in. The neighbors were shocked and full of forebodings, but it was a happy, busy home for my family.

Under my father's treatment through Yoga, diet, and herbal remedies, the Maharaja's health improved rapidly. Krishnamacharya soon became not only his Yoga teacher but also his friend and advisor, both on spiritual and political matters. In the beginning, it was Krishnamacharya's close relationship to the Maharaja that attracted students. These were mostly the children of palace officials, government ministers, and professional men. Soon, however, his evening lectures and Yoga demonstrations were attracting hundreds to Jaganmohan Palace. Obviously, his ability to stop his breath and heartbeat—always verified by a physician—caused a sensation. My father's fame spread further as a healer; he treated important government officials and anyone else who sought his help.

Long before dawn each morning, Krishnamacharya awakened, performed Yoga and private worship, and made his breakfast. Dressed very formally, he walked through the still-darkened streets to the palace for lessons at 4:30 A.M. First he taught the Maharaja and then each of his children. He would then go to the *Yogashala* where there would be classes, lectures, and administrative duties throughout the day and into the night. A few students also sought Krishnamacharya out for advanced teaching in sacred texts, such as the *Bhagavad Gita,* and, of course, he was closely if informally involved with the Parakala Math.

Looking back, it seems to me that the 1930s was an extraordinary decade in my father's life. It was also a crucial period for the continuation, perhaps the survival of the great tradition of Yoga that he represented.

Inspired by Mohandas K. Gandhi, our "Gandhiji," and led by the President of the Congress Party, Jawaharlal Nehru, India was moving irresistibly, if turbulently, toward independence. Equally powerful were the influences of Western modernism. For the emerging generation of the thirties it was a struggle not only against foreign domination, but also of the "new" against the "old."

Krishnamacharya did not favor independence. He did not agree with Gandhiji and with the pace of change, although several leading members of the Congress Party were students and friends. In my father's view, India had been ruled too long by outsiders and had not enough experience in self-government. He feared, prophetically, that too much of India's great cultural heritage would be swept aside by the forces of modernism and that politicians would become embroiled in religious strife. Whatever their faults, the British had seldom interfered with India's sacred traditions. For these reasons, my father belonged to the "old," one might even say "ancient," order of Indian life.

When I've talked to people who knew my father in the 1930s and go through the records of the *Yogashala,* I'm amazed at his prodigious efforts. Within a few years, he trained a few carefully chosen students as assistants and constantly attracted more to his classes. He also undertook lecture and demonstration tours through outlying districts and to more distant cities. Other maharajas called upon him as teacher and spiritual advisor. His classes were open to people of all ages, and from all walks of life, with financial help and encouragement for the poorest.

From the letters he received, it was apparent that my father attempted to reach his audiences on many levels, including the patriotic. A teacher at a physical-culture institute quoted my father as saying that ". . . Yoga not only gives strength to the body but to the mind also [which] is required for the all-sided development of any country," and that "the present miserable state of our nation is due to our neglect and indifference to this ancient system." And a judge observed that Krishnamacharya's "Yogic exercise is invaluable for the poverty-stricken Indian masses . . . indispensable for rural reconstruction."

The demonstrations were organized in schools, hospitals, even military installations where British officers were stationed. Through all of this, my father had the Maharaja's unstinting support. The Maharaja financed the *Yogashala* and lecture tours, and even decreed that Yoga should be taught in all the schools of Mysore state. He further instructed my father to write a series of books on Yoga.

According to my mother, the first book, *Yoga Makaranda,* was completed in seven days with my father working on it day and night. The King arranged for the photographs and the book was printed by the palace in 1934 and distributed for free. Soon, it was translated into several Indian languages. The *Yoga Makaranda* in our possession is incomplete because it was only the first of a series. Yet it is a fascinating work because it handled even very complex ideas with a clarity easily accessible to a general reader.

Krishnamacharya was during this period a staunch traditionalist. For example, he insisted that it was useless to cast a horoscope for a girl if she was unmarried by the age of puberty. He was also fiercely dedicated to his work. A perfectionist, he did not like to be argued with in his teaching. My mother said that people would run from his path as he walked down the street with his rapid, purposeful stride. They feared his temper, even his glare. When he and my mother would travel by train—always first class—the student teachers he brought along would stand the entire trip. They were afraid to sit in his presence. At the same time, he was always wonderful with children. He devised a particular way of teaching the young, called *vinyasa krama,* which is a continuous, energetic flow of movements because he knew they required animated exercise. Even when he lost his temper, there would be kind and loving words. Children were never afraid of him.

Two of Krishnamacharya's students during this period were of immense importance for the future of Yoga—and one of them he accepted only with the greatest reluctance.

The first was his brother-in-law, my uncle, B.K.S. Iyengar. He was only a teenager when he came to study with my father, and he was very serious, very devoted to Yoga. After a few years, Iyengar set out on his own and experienced severe hardships at first. In the late thirties, however, he was introduced to the famous violinist Yehudi Menuhin who was visiting India. The musician had experienced health problems, the most worrisome being tendonitis in one hand. Under Iyengar's teaching, his problem disappeared and Menuhin became a sincere, dedicated practitioner and advocate of Yoga.

Menuhin invited Iyengar to Europe where he introduced him to others who studied with him, some of whom later became teachers. My uncle was extraordinarily successful in spreading the message. His mastery of the most difficult *asanas* astonished Western audiences, and he was widely seen through films and photographs. He was also extremely effective in articulating the meaning of Yoga in his books, most notably *Light on Yoga,* which became a worldwide best-seller. Eventually, Iyengar established more than two hundred schools of Yoga around the world.

The student whom my father did not want to teach was an American woman married to a foreign diplomat. We know her now as Indra Devi. Then as now, she is an individual of remarkable imagination, energy, and purpose. She had started out to be a dancer, and had studied with Isadora Duncan. Through the writings of Madame Blavatsky and other founders of Theosophy, Indra Devi developed a deep interest in Indian philosophy. She was determined to study with Krishnamacharya.

He was equally determined that she would not. But she was a friend of the Maharaja, who urged my father to accept her as a student. Even my father's independence had limits; when the King insisted, he must be obeyed.

Krishnamacharya set rigorous standards of diet, conduct, and study for Indra. In time he appreciated her as one of his ablest students and closest friends. She, too, became one of the great teachers of the century. It is fair to say, I believe, that most students of Yoga today in the West have been influenced by the succeeding generations of teachers trained by Iyengar and Devi.

The Maharaja also called upon my father for guidance in other affairs that had nothing to do with Yoga. On occasion, huge European or American cars would arrive at our house, either with officials seeking advice or to carry Krishnamacharya to the palace. In those days, there were few automobiles in Mysore, so the neighbors called our home "the house of the cars." Many years later, my father told a French interviewer about one of the most difficult tasks he undertook for the Maharaja:

> I have participated in a great number of philosophical debates and discussions with all kinds of experts, but the debate with the Jains remains the most memorable.
>
> It was at Mysore, in 1930: one of my colleagues, Virupaksha Shastri of the College of Sanskrit, a member of a Shaivite sect, had long ago accomplished *vajapeya yajna,* a sacrificial rite of fertility and adoration of the sun, destined to ensure longevity and prosperity.
>
> The Maharaja had just offered a large sum of money to have this rite performed along the banks of the turbulent Tungabhadra river. But a group of Jains had arrived recently in the region. And upon hearing of the intended sacrifice they went out

among the throngs gathering along the river. It was here that the cow, with great pageantry, was being prepared for sacrifice. The Jains began stirring up the crowd with religious arguments against sacrifice.

Violence in general is considered forbidden by all Brahmins, but was not considered in this particular case because it was believed that this rite was specifically described in the sacred writings. The Jains, believing fanatically in their doctrine of bringing no violence of any kind to any living being (the non-violence of *ahimsa*), wanted the sacrifice stopped. When this potentially dangerous situation at the river became apparent, an official of the Maharaja sent me to intervene.

My wife reminded me that the *Bhagavad Gita* teaches that one does not have the right to avoid or turn away from one's duty. I went to the river to ask the Jains to leave.

Well aware of their reputation, I had asked for a police escort. I was well acquainted with the results of religious fanaticism. Just to be sure, we disguised the police with the sacred thread and facial markings, so that they appeared as disciples, and together we went to the river.

The situation was very overheated and dangerous, but a discussion was begun. Knowing that they were blinded by the passion of their beliefs, I reminded them that all of us held sacred respect for nonviolence, but that they, too, at times killed insects, scorpions, and serpents. I also gave them examples of times when violence was part of processes which led to a greater good. Such examples were child-birth, surgery, certain legal punishments, etc. I also reminded them that these results for the greater good were not only important physically, but psychologically and spiritually as well.

Regarding all of this, and in spite of their legendary pacifism, they carefully considered these ideas and responded by respecting the rights of those whose beliefs differed from their own. Once calm was restored, everyone agreed that by the discussion each group was allowed to hold and proclaim their views without robbing one another of the same.

Other than drawing upon his support for teaching, my father never sought advantage from his closeness to the Maharaja. At one point, the King offered my father a large piece of land, which he refused. A beautiful horse was sent as a gift—and sent back. Upon another occasion, the Maharanee, or Queen, gave some beautiful jewels to my father, and these, too, were returned. The only special favors he would accept were presents of fruit, vegetables, and flowers. Anything more valuable might lead to dependence, the loss of autonomy.

The fact that Krishnamacharya wasn't an opportunist did not spare him from palace jealousies. There were officials who spread rumors about him, and tried to discourage people from coming to our house. My father was unfazed. He often declared, "I cannot fail!" By this he meant that he could always stand on his own, with or without the support of the powerful.

My father's determination and independence were invaluable at the conclusion of the decade of the thirties. His friend Krishnaraja Wodejar died in 1940, and the heir to the throne had far less interest in Yoga. He studied personally with my father, and the school at Jaganmohan continued. But there was no longer financial support for publishing texts and sending teams of teachers to outlying towns and villages.

Meanwhile, our family had grown. The first child, my elder brother, was born in 1931. Just before my mother went into labor, my father undertook a pilgrimage to Tirupathi, to pray to the god Srinivasan. He returned just after my brother's birth, announcing before being told anything about it that his son's name was to be Srinivasan, after the god. Both the fact that he would have a son and his name had been foretold to my father in a dream. Between 1931 and 1952, my mother gave birth to three boys and three girls, and all of our names came to my father in dreams.

And so, my father was faithfully discharging the obligation to his guru—"to marry, raise children, and be a teacher of Yoga." Three times he was asked to become Swami of the Parakala Math, the supreme position held by his grandfather. Because of the promise he had made years earlier in Tibet, he always refused.

I was born in 1938, the second son. My earliest memories of a father are unlike those of most children because he was now entering his fifties. He seemed more like a grandfather. Also, he worked very hard and was usually away from home; it was left to my mother to do most of the child rearing. I remember Krishnamacharya as very strict. But I'm also reminded by people who knew us in those years that we children were quite naughty.

If your father is a professional athlete, you will naturally be expected to take part in sports, just as the child of a musician will seldom avoid music lessons. It follows that the son of a Yoga teacher will be required to do his prescribed exercises. One of my earliest memories is of refusing to do my *asanas* and dashing off. I was a very fast runner. When my father finally caught me, he got some rope and tied me into *padmasana,* one of the most basic seated postures, and left me for a while to think about it.

There are other early memories. My father was short, even by Indian standards, but he always seemed to be the tallest man in the room. He was exceptionally strong. When we went to a small farm in the countryside, I remember him carrying two heavy water jars, one on each shoulder, for three miles as if they were weightless. He dismayed relatives and neighbors by doing the most menial chores, unthinkable for a high-caste Brahmin, such as chopping wood and washing his own clothes. As I've said, even in the most conservative period in his life, Krishnamacharya had no use for castes.

His great love was gardening. Within the compound in front of our house he grew vegetables and flowers, which he would give to visiting relatives and friends. While gardening, he would teach his children Sanskrit. He was very devoted to our education, encouraging us to take advantage of modern ideas and Western science. Early on, I was having difficulty with English. Although it was a language in which my father had no interest, he took me aside and spent hours teaching me the English alphabet.

My father's rhythms of teaching, healing, and spiritual guidance in Mysore came to an abrupt end in 1947. India at long last achieved independence, and one of the first acts of the new political leaders locally was to dethrone the Maharaja. Not long afterwards, they shut down the *Yogashala.* Their action was not aimed at my father personally. In fact, the chief minister of the state, who cut off funds for the school, came to my father for treatment to help recover from an injury. It was so successful the official offered payment of five thousand rupees, a very large sum at that time. Krishnamacharya refused, saying: "I do not work for money. I do not need money. Give it to the poor students of the Yoga school!" But the school was too closely identified with the old order, which was to be swept aside. Even the state boundaries were redrawn as Mysore expanded into what is now Karnataka State.

My father calmly accepted the changes, including the loss of position and income. Once again he faced severe challenges. Entering his sixtieth year, he was forced to travel extensively to find students and to provide for his family and his children's education. I remember him coming home from these trips gray with fatigue, the only time I ever saw him appear less than perfectly healthy until great old age. Yet he never complained.

I was there when he gave his final lecture and demonstration at Jaganmohan Palace. There were hundreds of people in the vast hall, and his sentences in the purest classical Sanskrit flowed through the room like a majestic river. People were spellbound, even though hardly anyone in the room understood a word he said as the language was now in possession of very few. At the conclusion, as was his custom, Krishnamacharya singled out individuals to ask them questions based on his talk. I particularly admired one very clever fellow. Put on the spot, he shook his head slowly and said, "What you have said is so profound, Professor. I must think it over more carefully."

India's independence brought an end to a glorious period in my father's life. And it also brought a new beginning, a time of enormous changes for himself and for all who would come to study with him. Ever sustained by his faith in God, and dedicated to Yoga, Krishnamacharya could always proclaim: "I cannot fail!"

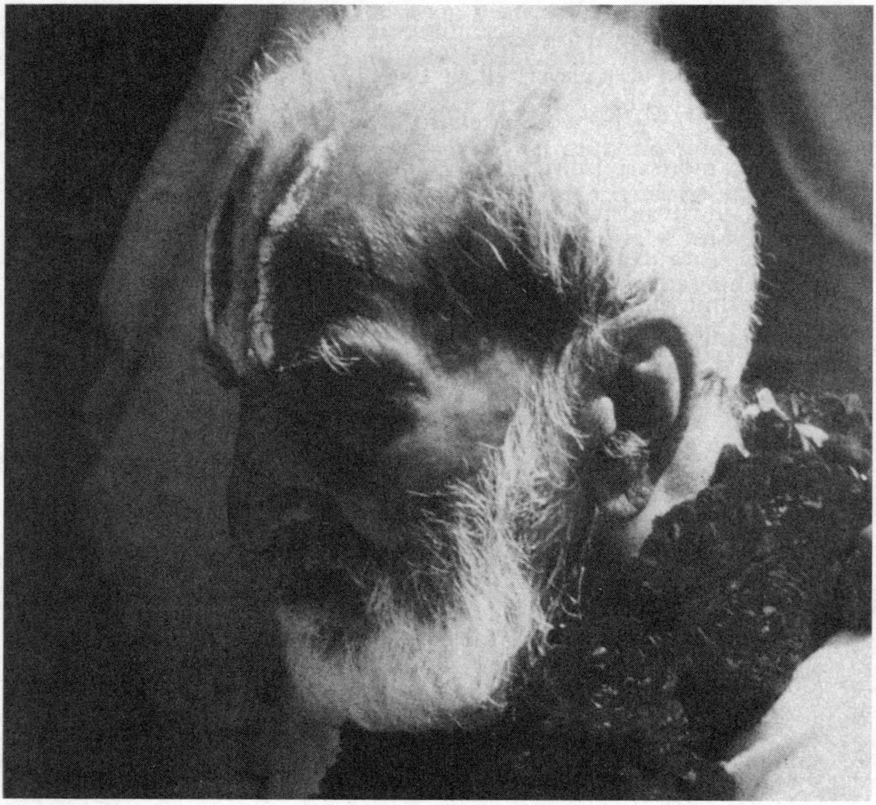

Krishnamacharya, Chennai, 1988

CHAPTER FIVE

A YOGIC VIEW OF HEALTH

Most important, according to me, is to provide necessary health, so that we can digest the food we eat, sleep well, and remember what we have been taught and what we have studied.

Looking upward into a clear night sky, the universe is laid out before our eyes. We see the brighter planets, the Polar star, and familiar constellations. Today, our vision is enhanced by telescopes, both earthbound and in orbit, which provide an astounding picture of events and objects in the farthest reaches of the cosmos.

We are also able to "listen" to the surrounding universe, thanks to radio telescopes developed in the twentieth century. Perceptions of radio waves have opened a new and entirely different way of understanding. In fact, when translated by computers into visual images, the sounds of the universe provide a startlingly different configuration of its makeup. Familiar imagery of constellations and galaxies disappear, and new and brilliant patterns emerge depicting a cosmos of sound.

The way we "see" and the way we "listen" to the universe are not incompatible. Just as the two senses enhance and expand our understanding of the immediate world, so do the two forms of astronomical observation enrich our study of a universe that has always drawn Mankind's wonder and awe.

This twofold ability to enquire into the infinite mysteries of the universe has its parallel—at least, metaphorically—in the way we may seek to understand our most intimate mystery: the human being. How are we formed, how do we function? What is the source of our physical and mental suffering, and how are we brought back to well-being? What are the limits, if any, of our capabilities? What is our place in this vast universe, God's measureless creation—and how do we assume it?

Obviously, no one can offer definite answers to these questions. But for anyone inclined toward such inquiries, we live in a most fortunate age. We have at our disposal two different approaches to our questions: the intellectual accomplishments and extraordinary tools of modern science, coexisting with a legacy of thousands of years of human experience and its divinely inspired, hard-won wisdom. In short, we have two broadly conceived ways of observing the human being.

When the subject of our study is health, we now conventionally describe the "modern," "scientific" approach as *allopathic,* and the ancient yet very contemporary methods as *traditional.* They are not mutually exclusive, as increasing numbers of open-minded health practitioners of each approach are coming to recognize. Like the ability to see and to hear, allopathic and traditional systems can be mutually reinforcing and beneficial.

At the same time, it must be admitted that it is not easy for an individual trained for years in one system to absorb and integrate another. It is rather like someone who has thought, spoken, and written English all his life attempting to master Sanskrit, or vice versa. I know this from personal experience. My education and early mental equipment were completely oriented toward Western science and technology when I first approached my father and asked him to teach me. For his part, Krishnamacharya was frankly dubious about having me as a student.

To explain how this came about, let me pick up the thread of Krishnamacharya's story after his departure from Mysore.

For a couple of years, he made his base in Bangalore. In this beautiful city, a few hundred kilometers east of Mysore, he continued to teach and to heal, but it remained very difficult for him. Bangalore is one of India's most future-oriented cities—today the center of one of the world's vital industries for advanced computer software. During those early years of India's independence and its rush to create a modern, industrial nation, there weren't many students eager to study ancient traditions with an aging Yogi. In 1952, however, one of India's most distinguished jurists, who had helped frame our constitution, invited Krishnamacharya to relocate to Chennai. The great lawyer sought my father's help in recovering from a stroke, and he was joined by other leading citizens who wanted to take advantage of Krishnamacharya's renowned healing skills.

My father accepted the invitation, and was ever after grateful to the people of Chennai. He was now consulted primarily as a healer, although he continued to meet with visiting scholars and those few who sought him out for more serious study of Yoga.

Chennai was an ideal setting for Krishnamacharya. It is India's fourth largest city, a busy seaport on the Bay of Bengal from which trade is exchanged with all parts of the world. At the same time, Chennai, which is the capital of the state of Tamil Nadu, is an invigorating center of spiritual, artistic, and intellectual endeavor—and has been so for many centuries. Tolerance and a genuine spirit of inquiry prevail. It was here that Jesus's skeptical disciple known as Doubting Thomas came to found his mission: a beautiful Christian church marks the spot where he is said to have died. Hindu, Muslim, Buddhist, Jain, and virtually every other religious adherent have, except for very rare occasions, coexisted here peaceably and in mutual respect. It is in Chennai that Annie Besant founded the worldwide center of the Theosophical Society, and the city is filled with institutions of learning—from the great University of Madras to technical and vocational schools to colleges that teach ancient languages. There are schools devoted to the preservation and perpetuation of art, dance, and theater, and centers dedicated to the teachings of such revered sages as Ramakrishna and Vivekananda.

In Chennai, Krishnamacharya, who was now in his sixties, established a very simple household and went on with his teaching, healing, study, and worship. He also underwent, in the eyes of those who had known him in Mysore, a startling transformation. Previously, his general reputation had been intimidating—people found his strictness and temper fearsome. He retained the strictness, at least as far as rigorously maintaining both his personal standards and the practice of individuals who came to him as students. But the strictness was tempered by a gentleness and kindliness that astonished some of his old friends and family members. To put it simply, Krishnamacharya mellowed. People who knew his kindness and his tranquil, even playful disposition in later life found it difficult to believe that he once had such a terrifying reputation.

For my part, I had remained in Mysore to study at the university and take a degree in mechanical engineering. It was a course of study of which my family fully approved. Most of my friends were also studying to be engineers, so it seemed a sociable choice. After graduation, I easily found a good job and was soon about to be transferred to northern India. On a visit to my parents, however, my father asked why I didn't stay and work in Chennai. It seemed like a good idea. I liked the city and its people as he did and I wanted to be close to my family. With the help of some of my father's contacts, I quickly found another job with a Danish firm and also took up residence.

It was a very enjoyable life. I had a good job, status, and a wonderful social life—my mother always felt that I had too many friends.

My father was very pleased for me. Then, one day, the most remarkable thing happened.

I was visiting my parents, and sitting with my father outside their small home. A large American car drove up, barely able to squeeze through the narrow street. Out jumped a large, middle-aged woman in a brightly colored dress. She ran up to my father, threw her arms around him in a big hug, and shouted, "Thank you, Professor! Thank you so much!"

To see a tall woman from New Zealand embracing a small, elderly, half-naked Brahmin would have been startling in itself. But to anyone who knew my father, such behavior was unthinkable. Yet, he simply smiled and treated her graciously. After she left, I asked my father what had happened.

"She's suffered from insomnia," he said. "She could barely sleep even with powerful drugs. She's been studying with me and just said that she was having her first nights of good sleep in more than twenty years."

I was fascinated. I'd known of my father's reputation as a healer, of course, but had seldom seen it so dramatically expressed at firsthand.

"Father," I said, "I want to know more about this. You must teach me."

He was very reluctant. He knew that I had a busy professional and social life. I suspect that he believed I was asking out of idle curiosity, that I wasn't sincere. But I persisted. It was always part of Krishnamacharya's deepest ethic that no student should be turned away, provided that he or she was sincere. To test me, he set difficult conditions. I would have to arrive to study with him at precisely three o'clock every morning. He was always a stickler for absolute punctuality with all of his students. To be even a minute or two late would terminate our lessons. And I would have to study with complete attention and dedication.

I, too, had a condition. I told Krishnamacharya that I wanted to study the *Yoga Sutras*, but without religion—no prayers, mantras, or mention of God. He agreed readily. As I've said, Krishnamacharya found no difficulty in being simultaneously the most devout and the most tolerant of men.

And so, in September 1961, I began studies with my father that would last almost to the final hours before he sank into a coma and then death twenty-eight years later.

Since it is my purpose to sketch in broad outline the principle concepts and practices pertaining to Yoga, I can only hint at the range of our studies. Generally, they took three forms. First, there were the studies of *asanas, pranayama,* and related physical practice, which might require three or more hours a day. Second, there were the studies of the most important historical texts and commentaries related to Yoga. These later were followed by texts from the *Vedas, Upanishads,* and other spiritual, philosophical, and literary works. Each of these had to be memorized perfectly, after which my father would provide explanations. Finally, there would be note-taking and reading of works that he assigned. There was a great deal of information imparted concerning diagnosis, diet, and Ayurvedic practice, including the use of herbal remedies and oils.

In the course of these studies, I learned what my father meant when he described himself as a student of Yoga—never as *Yogin,* or master. He, too, was always studying, exploring, and experimenting. This was particularly true in the last third of his life. In Mysore, he had been tremendously busy with the school and his duties for the Maharaja. In Chennai, he had more time to devote to scholarship. Outwardly, he had mellowed; inwardly, I believe he was even more restlessly curious and creative the older he grew.

Looking back, I'm not sure that I would have embarked on these studies if I had had any idea of what an enormous amount of knowledge he had to impart. One of the reasons my father had so few long-term students in his life was that there was simply too much information. It was daunting. But he had the gift of knowing just what each student was prepared to learn at any given point. When we went through the *Yoga Sutras* the first time, which took four years, he never once mentioned God or any religious associations. This was to change, of course, in our subsequent six passages through Patanjali's great work in the decades that followed.

My initial problem, as I've said, was simply to make the enormous intellectual leap into Krishnamacharya's tradition—into concepts and ideas that seemed completely alien. To give just one example: It is axiomatic in Western physiology that the heart pumps blood that enables other organs to perform their function, including the lungs—in other words, the heart pumps the lungs. In Krishnamacharya's system, the lungs are the pump that makes the heart work. It defies all we know, and yet it is a basic concept that works as part of a total, integrated system of concepts based upon conscious involvement of breath, body, and mind. We each know firsthand that we can lower the rate of heartbeat by regulating the breath. Does that make the modern, scientific view of the heart's function incorrect? Absolutely not. Equally, Krishnamacharya's concept of the lungs as the primary pump has practical and profound implications within his system of Yoga. As I've suggested, it's rather like "seeing" and "listening" to the universe: two totally different systems of observation and interpretation, each valuable within the proper context.

The biggest help that I had in making the transition into my father's tradition came unintentionally from my younger brother. Sribhasyam had been studying with my father before I had, and he, too, had a Western education. Through the door, I would hear loud arguments. My brother would quote Freud, for example, and protest against something my father said about the mind. Then, I would hear my father shouting back. I decided that if I were to learn from my father I would have to open my mind, stifle the doubts and confusions, and accept what he had to teach on his terms. Nothing was to be gained by pitting Freud against Patanjali. By willing myself to adapt, I also experienced one of the most profound lessons of Yoga—for Yoga is about openness.

With this in mind, let me lay out in the most general terms a Yogic view of the human system and how it works. I must caution the reader that this is a very simplistic rendering of an extremely complex subject. It is rather like identifying the skeleton and major organs on an anatomical chart as indicating the scientific view of how the human organism works—a study that in fact entails a medical vocabulary of more than a quarter of a million words. What I am attempting to do is to illustrate the coherent nature of Yogic concepts, particularly as they involve the basic elements of *asana* and *pranayama*.

As Patanjali relates, God as Ishvara dwells within each of us, and our personal conduit is through the *purusha*, the indwelling eternal Perceiver. The *purusha*, however, perceives only through the mind. "Mind" is an elusive term. In Sanskrit it is called *chitta*, which indicates—as I've described more fully in Chapter Three—the activities that compose it. These are comprehension, misapprehension, imagination, deep sleep, and memory.

In the Yogic system, the mind is considered located in the heart region. This might have something to do with the tradition of learning through sound—the chanting voice of the teacher. Interestingly, in the West one refers to rote memorization as "learning by heart."

A more fundamental premise of our system is that mind and body are inseparable. The mind perceives through the senses, and these are conceived as capacities both of perception and action. The senses of perception are familiar: hearing, feeling, seeing, tasting, smelling. The senses of action are vocal, manual, locomotion, evacuation, and generation.

There is a duality in this system, although not of body and mind. It is the distinction between the *purusha*, which is eternal and changeless, and everything else that composes the natural world, which is constantly changing. All that changes is embraced by the term *prakriti*, and it includes mind, body, senses and every being and everything that exists in the external world. And *prakriti*, as the *Yoga Sutras* teach, is constantly subject to the interplay of the three *gunas*—*tamas* (heaviness), *rajas* (frenetic activity), and *sattva* (clarity).

If we comprehend that everything we experience is subject to change, then we also appreciate the great possibilities opened by the *Yoga Sutras*: everything can be modified in a chosen way.

Directed change is possible because we have unlimited energy at our disposal in the form of *prana*. It means "that which is constantly present everywhere." Many other definitions are offered, such as "life force," "deified breath," and cosmic "life of the world."

An eloquent description of *prana* was offered by Swami Vivekananda, a world teacher whose appearance at the 1893 Parliament of Religions held in Chicago was a crucial event in awakening Western interest in the ancient wisdom of India.

"*Prana*," he wrote, "is the infinite, omnipresent manifesting power of this universe . . . out of this *prana* is evolved everything that we call force. It is *prana* that is manifesting as gravitation, as magnetism. It is *prana* that is manifesting as actions of the body, as the nerve currents, as thought-force. . . . The sum total of all forces in the universe, mental or physical, when resolved back to their original state is called *prana*."

In my father's teaching, *prana* radiated out from the body and beyond as an expression of the *purusha*. Since the *purusha* perceives only through the mind, there is an intimate relationship between *prana*, mind, and breath—the means through which we can consciously regulate the flow of this energy. We thus view an agitated mind, which can lead to illness, as one that has dispersed *prana* beyond the body. True health is the unimpeded flow and containment of *prana* within the body.

Prana enters the body and is distributed through passages called *nadis*. There are 72,000 *nadis*, but two that spiral upward through the trunk around the spine are of primary importance: one starting on the left and terminating on the right, called *ida*; the other starting on the right and terminating on the left, called *pingala*. The *ida* and *pingala* intersect at six points. These are: the eyebrow, at the throat, somewhere in the middle of the heart, at the navel, just above the base of the trunk, and at the base of the spine. These intersections correspond to the *chakras,* those places in the body that are represented in so many religious and philosophical systems of the East. The *chakras* help determine the nature of Yogic practice by guiding concentration and action in specific ways—for example, toward the heart region, where the indwelling *prana* is centered, or toward the navel area, *agni,* which represents fire.

One other *nadi* of vital importance is the *shushumna,* the central channel that extends through the body. Normally, *prana* can enter the body only through the *ida* or *pingala,* but the ideal placement of *prana* is directed into the *shushumna.* When the *prana* is contained within the *shushumna,* it is not outside the body, and an individual is described as in a state of health—a state of Yoga. When *prana* is not within the *shushumna,* it is because there is an obstacle blocking its passage. Impurities that we bring into the body are among the chief obstacles. They tend to concentrate in the lower region of the abdomen and are known, succinctly, as *apanas*: "dirt."

The greatest obstacle preventing the entry of *prana* into the *shushumna* is *kundalini. Kundalini* is located near the base of the spine between the lowest two *chakras.* In what is sometimes known as *Kundalini Yoga,* it takes the image of a coiled serpent. Through meditation and sometimes violent breath exercises, the serpent is said to rise through the spine releasing explosive energy. My father saw it differently. To Krishnamacharya, *kundalini* was a blockage—the nucleus of imbalance in the body. Through proper practice, it was released to permit the flow of *prana.*

In the simplest terms, *asanas,* or postures, are designed to open the *nadis. Pranayama* enables us to increase *prana* within us and direct it as a cleansing force that eliminates impurities. They are the principle methods that strengthen and interact with all other elements of Yoga: our relationships with others, our personal discipline, and the ability ultimately to direct our minds in such a way that unleashes new powers of comprehension and change.

We are told that when Lord Shiva created Yoga, there were eighty-four million *asanas,* one for each man and woman then living upon the earth. Today, we have at most only a few hundred known postures at our disposal. One definition of *asana* is "to place the different parts of the body in unusual positions." Some appear quite simple, such as sitting cross-legged or standing, stretching the arms overhead, then slowly bending forward. Others are more difficult, such as the headstand and shoulder stand. And there are *asanas* of such complexity that they seem to defy the limits of physical possibility.

Properly executed, all programs of *asana* will help increase muscular strength and tone, improve flexibility, remove impurities, and provide many other benefits. It cannot be sufficiently emphasized, however, that *asanas* must be learned from a competent teacher over a sustained period of time. Improperly performed, Yogic postures can weaken and even harm an individual.

What differentiates *asana* from other forms of physical exercise? Perhaps the most important distinction is the conscious involvement of the mind in the movement and the placement of the body. Yoga can be enormously helpful to sports enthusiasts, but it should always be considered a separate activity. There is no competition with others: it is the unique development of the individual according to his or her needs and abilities.

There are many classes of *asana,* such as standing, sitting, lying, inverted, forward bending, back bending, and twisting. When properly chosen and organized into a sequence, every part of the body is exercised in every direction. In fact, the ideal exercise plan must ensure that all joints from toes to fingertips, all sections of the body, and the respiratory and circulatory systems are adequately "felt" and exercised.

Perhaps more than any other teacher of Yoga, my father emphasized the importance of bringing *pranayama* into the practice of *asana.* Previously, the convention was to perform a sequence of postures, then assume a comfortable position for a prolonged period of breath exercise. Krishnamacharya felt that long, smooth inhalations, exhalations, and moments of retention were essential to the union of body, mind, and breath. Inhalations normally accompany stretches and backward bending, while exhalations belong to the contracted, forward bending motions. In fact, breath is the measure of results. If, at the end of a program of exercise, the student is breathing hard or the pulse is accelerated, the rhythm and sequence of movement has been too energetic.

The practice of *asanas* prepares the body and mind naturally for *pranayama*. The student assumes a seated position, on a chair or cross-legged upon the floor, so that the dorsal spine straightens comfortably. The posture must have the qualities of any well-executed *asana*, namely the duality of stability and alert relaxation prescribed in the *Yoga Sutras*.

Along with inhalation, exhalation, and retention, techniques of *pranayama* scrupulously conform to the placement of breath within the body—for example, drawing air into the upper chest or deep into the region of the diaphragm. The number of breaths and the ratio of duration is equally important. Special attention is given to exhalation because it facilitates calming of the mind.

As suggested, *asanas* are needed to open the *nadis*; *pranayama* is what brings *prana* into contact with *apana*, or dirt, and so removes impurities. The dual effect is a progressive increase of inner *prana* and with it the development of mental tranquillity and clarity, the closer engagement of mind and *purusha*.

There are many techniques of *pranayama*, and they, too, must be carefully taught. The benefits are immediately felt, and in the long run almost defy description. But consider this, the ancients taught that each individual is allotted 21,600 breaths per day in a life span intended to be one hundred years long. We can draw upon our allotted breaths like a bank account. Through anxiety, short breaths, and unnecessary exertion we may overdraw our account—and so shorten our lives. Or we may use the breath wisely, with smooth, easy respiration, and store it up: in other words, lengthen our lives. Incidentally, the first few hundred breaths taken after waking each day are dedicated to Ganesh—the beloved elephant-headed god of new beginnings, the remover of obstacles, the enabler. In this way, we bring the breath consciously into a daily act of renewal.

In the practice of Yoga for health, there is a third element that must be introduced. This is the practice of self-study that accompanies *asanas* and *pranayama,* and it is known by the general term, *dhyana.*

Our lives are almost entirely governed by our actions and their consequences. As the *Yoga Sutras* state, any action can reveal its results immediately or in the course of time; those results can be good or bad, and they are part of a continuous process—one action influencing another ad infinitum. *Dhyana* is the quiet meditation, the reflection we bring to the consideration of action. One example is the so-called "worst case scenario." We reach a firm decision about something we are to do, but before acting we reflect upon the possible negative effects. Whether we leave our decision unaltered or changed in some fashion, the reflection helps bring clarity of mind and precision of action.

As we have discovered, all Yogic practice is aimed at reducing *avidya,* the film that covers the mind, and the resulting *dukha,* the restrictions that hinder our actions. As we bring steady observation and inquiry of the self into our practice, we reduce *avidya* as a matter of course.

Among my father's enduring contributions was his ability to express the theory and practice of Yoga in concrete, practical terms. He discarded even the most sanctified past teaching if he felt that it was unclear or unhelpful. He chose aspects of Yoga that he had found through trial and error to be most suitable in the modern world. Krishnamacharya's task was to bring all that he knew into a coherent system.

In designing a practice, an immediate consideration was the age of the individual. Unless there were physical problems, children were to concentrate on *asanas* performed in rapid, energetic sequence: otherwise, they would get bored. With maturity, the emphasis shifted more to *pranayama* and *dhyana,* while elderly practitioners were to devote the greater portion of their efforts toward *dhyana.*

Yogic practice is also designed according to the needs and wishes of the student. There are three general strategies for pursuing constant effort and attention in a single direction:

- Strengthening body and mind;
- Curing illness by removing impurities; and
- Understanding the higher force by focusing, then merging the mind on the object of contemplation.

Place and physical conditions are also important. In his writings from the 1930s, Krishnamacharya advised students to avoid practicing *asanas* in the jungle, where there were biting insects, serpents, and dangerous animals. This is hardly a problem for most students many years later, and he would adapt the advice for contemporary urban conditions. Oddly, there are still teachers who find it difficult to free themselves from what they believe are hard and fast rules. Once, when I was in Switzerland, there was a teacher who used to organize classes very early in the morning. We were located at an altitude of 1,500 meters and in a cold climate. In Chennai, where it is tropical and very hot, early morning classes are ideal. Unfortunately, the Swiss teacher extended this schedule to his own locale and as a result, many students fell ill. Yogic practice should occur in a setting that is as comfortable as possible: clean, quiet, and conducive to concentration.

The concept that guides the performance of an *asana* and also the course of practice is called *vinyasa.* It means step-by-step, a progression that has a beginning, middle, and end. When applied to a particular posture, *vinyasa* begins with visualization, proceeds to the starting position and the incorporation of the breath into the movement. The *asana* is per-

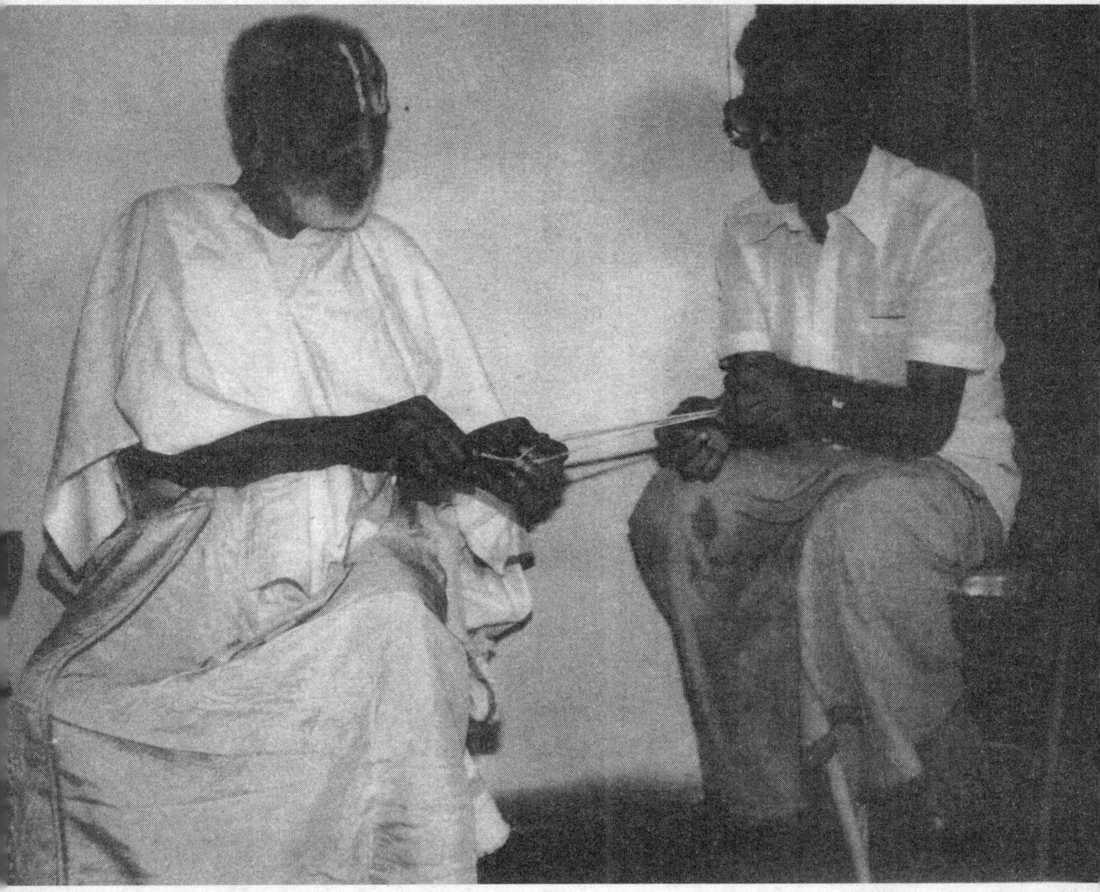

PREVIOUS PAGE:
Krishnamacharya at the age of ninety-nine, Chennai, April 1987

LEFT:
Krishnamacharya at his centenary celebration with Indra Devi at his residence in Chennai, 1988

ABOVE:
Krishnamacharya and Desikachar, Chennai, 1988

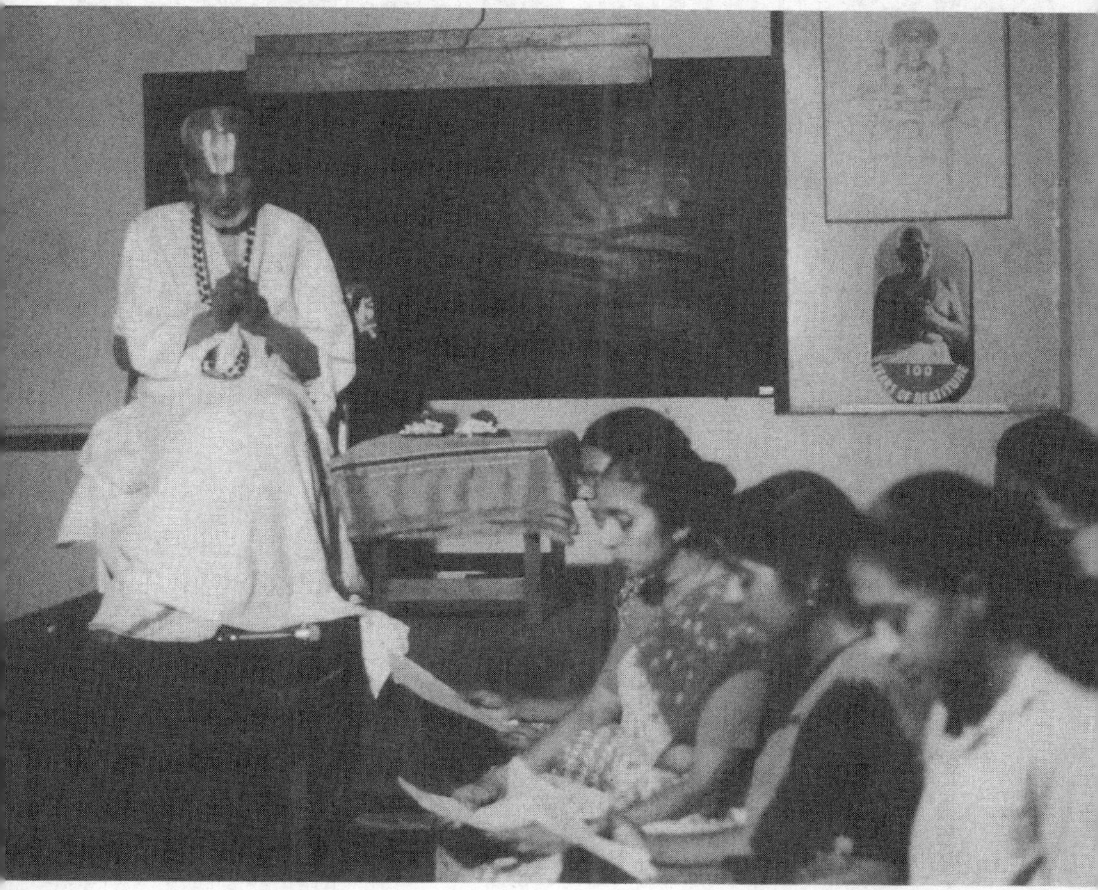

Photographs by Pierre Courtejoie

ABOVE:

Krishnamacharya conducting a chanting class with his students at the Krishnamacharya Yoga Mandiram, Chennai, 1988

LEFT:

Krishnamacharya addressing a gathering, 1988

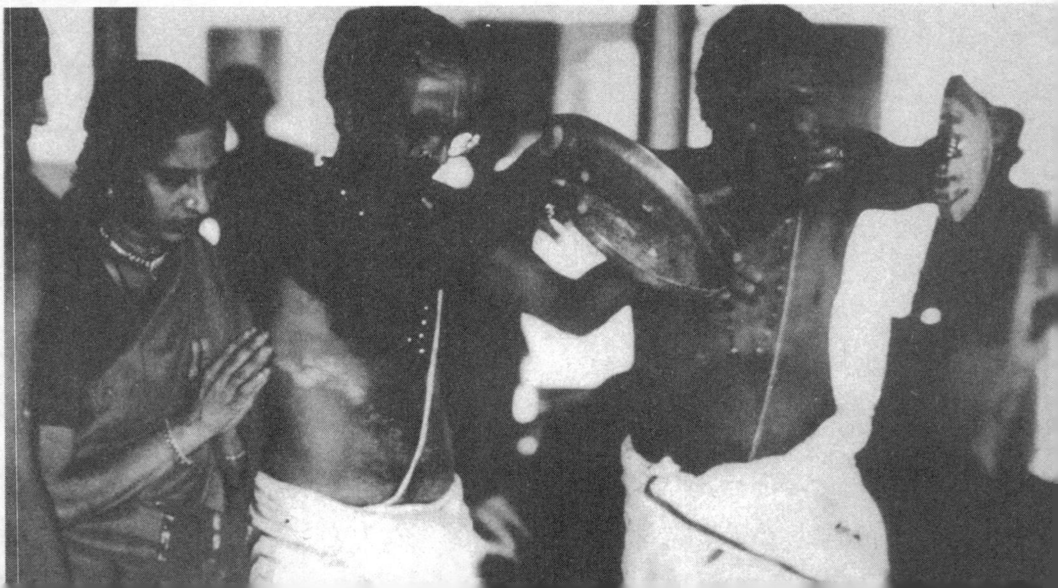

LEFT TOP:
Krishnamacharya's centenary celebration at the Sringeri Math, Chennai, 1988.

LEFT BOTTOM:
The conclusion of the centenary celebration at the Sringeri Math, Chennai, 1988

ABOVE:
Krishnamacharya at the Centenary Celebration at the Sringeri Math, Chennai, 1988

FOLLOWING PAGE:
Krishnamacharya, Chennai, 1984

formed with concentration on the flow of the movement and smoothness of inhalation, exhalation, and often retention of breath, and toward the prescribed completion.

Each step is a preparation for the next. And so it is with the sequence of *asanas.* Each posture is part of a flow of exercise: a beginning, a building toward a posture that is the height of the program, and then a progression toward an ending.

Vinyasa is, I believe, one of the richest concepts to emerge from Yoga for the successful conduct of our actions and relationships. My father's students were often amazed that he would greet them at the gate when they arrived, conduct the lessons, and then escort them back to the gate and bid them farewell. It is a practice that I continue. Often, a student considers it a somewhat elaborate courtesy, but it is actually *vinyasa.* Our time together begins with their arrival and draws to a close with the departure. *Vinyasa* grants both teacher and student a sense of completion that is also a preparation for the next phase of our life. For me, perhaps, it is the arrival of another student; for the student it might be time to start thinking about an appointment, or returning to family chores or a job.

In *vinyasa,* the ending of a progression takes on deep meaning. The last *asana* must be close to what we do next. If I am moving toward *pranayama,* I'll want to be in a sitting position. If I am planning to sleep, the final posture must not be something that keeps me awake but, rather, a position in a lying position. *Vinyasa* is in itself a form of self-study that engages attention upon the consequences of our actions. When we devote all of our concentration, energy, and time to a special work project, we must know how to bring it to a close and resume the normal rhythms of work and family life.

Another element that my father emphasized is compensation. There are asymmetric postures such as twists of the trunk while extending a leg. They can tend to have negative effects unless there is a compensatory movement. This simple concept has its parallels in other aspects of life.

Too often, our actions struggle toward extraordinary results without regard for compensating effort.

I have two brothers. When we were children there was a very tall coconut tree in our yard. My older brother said he knew how to climb tall trees, so my other brother and I challenged him to do it. I distinctly remember taunting him: "Go up, go up, go up!" He climbed the tree, but then he did not know how to come down. There was no one to help him, so he remained up there quite a while. That is what is meant by compensation. It is not enough to know how to climb a tree; we must also know how to come back down. When we do a headstand, we must know how to come back down to a normal position without problems. When we act toward or beyond our limits, compensation restores balance, harmony.

"I was first initiated into Yoga by my parents . . . in the daily ritual of taking food." If the reader will recall that remark from my father's autobiographical sketch (Chapter Two), then the enormous importance Krishnamacharya placed upon food in relationship to health will be evident. "In this context, *Yoga* means *to join*. Something outside joins in me, whether it is mother's milk or the food we take."

In all times, in all places, food is a universal concern of Mankind—the inspiration of myth, the early foundation of social organization, and the subject of countless rules, rituals, and recipes. In India, as in much of the world where history has been marked by famine, hunger is the overriding concern of millions. And I must admit we are at times dismayed by the enormous resources devoted in the West to the problem of *too much* food—the billions of dollars and obsessive attention devoted to dieting. In this sense, both the hungry and the overfed have at least one thing in common: a preoccupation with food.

Annam is a Sanskrit word with dual meanings: "The food that nourishes" and "the food that consumes." The food that nourishes brings harmony of body and mind, provides energy for clarity in thought and action, fuels true health. The food that "consumes," of course, does the opposite. When all of our attention is directed toward food—whether the problem is too much or too little—our lives are taken over by this one aspect of existence. Even in the normal flow of life, food exercises a powerful, perhaps not altogether appreciated, influence over our mind and emotions.

Let me emphatically clear up one widespread misunderstanding. Nowhere in the Vedas or in the ancient teachings is it said that you must be a strict vegetarian. Westerners, in particular, seem to believe that to seriously study Yoga it is imperative to adopt a vegetarian life-style. This is not the case, and for some individuals may even be unhealthy. That my family has a vegetarian diet is a matter of preference, but we live in a hot, tropical climate that produces a great abundance and variety of fruits, grains, and vegetables. To choose to be a vegetarian may indeed be essential to health for some individuals—or a matter of taste, environmental conviction, philosophy, or religious belief. But it is not a commandment embedded in Yoga.

What is the proper attitude toward food, the ideal diet?

Krishnamacharya's teachings on the subject often come as a surprise. Although there were certain guidelines based upon common sense, he taught that food—as all other aspects of Yoga—must be considered in terms of the individual. We must begin to understand our needs and responses to food with the same care we devote to an understanding of our bodies, mind, and breath. It is an integral part of our self-study.

In some cases, it is apparent. For example, I cannot drink coffee; my wife has a terrible reaction to almonds—yet she drinks coffee and I can eat all the almonds I want. Allergic reactions, then, are one of the more accessible ways to comprehend our relationship to food. More difficult to grasp fully, though no less influential, is cultural conditioning and the role of the senses. We develop a taste for certain foods that we interpret as needs: When we can't have them, we feel deprived and once again thoughts of food dominate our minds.

According to our system, the individual is subject to the interplay of the three qualities that pervade all of existence, the *gunas*: *tamas* (heaviness), *rajas* (frenetic activity), and *sattva* (clarity).

The three *gunas* likewise apply to food, and a little reflection will tell us how much we already know about their nature from personal experience. *Tamasic* foods—such as red meat, or sauces rich in cream, butter and cheese—induce a feeling of heaviness. *Rajasic* foods provide heightened stimulation for the system; even as we eat, say, a hot and spicy meal we can feel the body temperature rise. *Sattvic* foods, such as simply prepared legumes or green vegetables, tend to sustain and enrich our energies without distorting them.

In general terms, we understand the effects of the foods we eat. We know that a late supper that includes chillies and pungent spices is likely to keep us awake, just as a "heavy" meal makes us drowsy. As part of Yogic practice, we attempt to increase our sensitivity to food—not through general rules of dieting but through consciousness of our own experiences. For example, we reflect upon the power of the senses that tell us we hunger for sweets or fried foods. The focus shifts to our emotional states. Do we feel heavy-minded and slow-witted? Our system may be calling for *rajasic* food. Is our mind too busy with thoughts for relaxation or sleep? The classic example of a glass of warm milk before going to bed may be the *tamasic* solution. Do we feel the need for sustained, clear-minded action throughout the afternoon? A midday meal of simply cooked vegetables may be the *sattvic* necessity. In sum, we undertake to redefine our diet in terms of constantly changing individual needs for physical vitality, clarity of mind, and balanced emotions.

It is one thing to understand these needs, quite another to make the necessary changes. In some instances, an abrupt change in food habits may be a matter of emergency. For example a physician perceives dangerous levels of fat in a patient's system, or a newly diagnosed diabetic's urgent need to reduce sugar intake. In most cases, however, abrupt changes in such deeply instilled habits as our relationship to food do not seem to be very helpful.

A Yoga student at the Mandiram was experiencing health problems and went to an Ayurvedic physician in Chennai. This practitioner prescribed a drastic change in the woman's cooking techniques and diet. No food was to be cooked in the gas oven, but only over charcoal. Only copper vessels were to be used. And each meal was to be very slowly cooked, for as long as three hours. It may have been sound advice, but the woman, who was asthmatic, had a very small, enclosed kitchen. The charcoal cooking proved to be a problem. Also, she had a career and small children: she simply did not have three hours a day to cook meals. After a couple of days, she abandoned the entire regimen. Please understand, I have enormous respect for Ayurveda, but it seems that in this instance the prescription was too drastic and not tailored to the woman's individual needs. And we encounter similar situations in the West where people undertake "crash diets" or other dramatic changes and deprivations.

Similarly, although respecting the religious associations, my father did not encourage fasting. Krishnamacharya taught that we should eat when we are hungry, and always leave one-quarter of the stomach empty. Incidentally, he also taught that four hours should elapse between a heavy meal and Yogic practice.

How do we begin to change our eating habits so that food nourishes, rather than consumes us? Once again, the ancients had a very practical approach. They knew that rich cooking smells can awaken appetites and draw us like magnets. So they always placed the *puja* room, where religious worship and sacrifice occurs, right next to the dining area. The effect was to remind us that food is taken for more than its own sake. It is an offering to the gods through our nourishment. Also, the ancients advised beginning a meal with only a few sips of water and a few grains or rice. This had the practical effect of awakening the stomach for easy digestion, and also to ease hunger pangs so that one would not simply plunge into eating. This might be described as exactly the opposite of a fast-food restaurant where, in Western slang, the diner "digs in." Traditionally, the meal would progress toward the main dishes, then end with a small amount of sweets and soothing curd, or yogurt.

The ancient practice, then, was to structure a meal with a beginning, climax, and end—and it was the same with approaches to changes in diet. It would always begin with small increments. If someone with a taste for lemons is also having stomach problems, we don't tell them to eliminate lemons immediately. We recommend eliminating a lemon a day, then perhaps more. Or there is the gradual replacement of one food for another, of boiled rice for a fried potato.

Such practices, of course, arise out of the basic nature of Yoga—gradually arriving at a place we have not been before. It is also the more specific practice that I've mentioned, of *vinyasa*: the planned progression of a course of action.

Such practices become easier as we learn to understand, to feel, to "listen" to the experience of our bodies through *asana*, *pranayama*, and *dhyana*. Food is part of the continuous striving toward unity. And it will be a very individual experience.

Krishnamacharya was a superb cook, especially of the hot and spicy foods of southern India. Also, he would eat enormous amounts of sweets—literally taking them throughout the day. I was always amazed by it. I can only surmise that all of his other Yogic practices made it possible, but I've never met anyone else who could do it.

Proper exercise, regulated breath, self-study, nourishing food—these are the basic constituents of health in Yoga. And we immediately recognize that they are universal and ageless prescriptions in all traditions of healing, including the most modern allopathic medical sciences. Yet, there are profound, complementary differences between allopathic and Yogic approaches to health.

It is the genius of modern science to approach the individual from the outside, from the standpoint of the problem. This is the very meaning of allopathic—to differentiate, analyze, and test rigorously for specific cures. Because of this approach, some of mankind's ancient scourges have been eliminated—the last cases of smallpox were recorded in India before the World Health Organization reported that this hideous disease had been defeated. It is impossible to overstate the contributions of modern science in ending suffering and restoring health.

Yoga approaches the individual from the inside, through the mind. Yet each individual is not simply a mind, but a system. Actually, each of us is a conglomeration of a vast system. This system is more than my body, which is nourished by food. It is more than my breath, more than my relationships, more than my faith. Any influence upon one aspect of the system will affect every other aspect. What we experience in Yoga is a conscious influence and change in the overall system. We may choose to begin with the body, the breath, our food, or our relationships. Whatever the point of beginning, we change the totality of the system. It is impossible to overstate the possibilities of this gradual approach to well-being in our lives.

For those who choose to look, the wisdom of the world's ancient healing traditions is at their disposal—even as the human mind ventures into the beneficial frontiers of scientific medicine. It is within our capacity to be the healthiest humans who have ever lived on this planet.

Krishnamacharya Teaching a Student Uttanasana, *Chennai, 1954*

CHAPTER SIX

THE NATURE OF HEALING

Illness is an obstacle on the road to spiritual enlightenment. That is why you have to do something about it.

Healing is as ordinary a human experience as it is mysterious. From the moment of birth, we suffer discomforts, diseases, and injuries. Whether these are episodes or chronic conditions, whether minor or life-threatening, there is an inner power of recovery and restoration at work—even up to the final moments of life. Healing is a natural gift. The quest to understand, awaken, and enhance this gift, both in ourselves and in others, is among the more self-interested and generous human efforts.

Every culture that has ever existed has undertaken this quest. In our time, as I've suggested, we are extremely fortunate. If we are wise enough, we can bring together accumulated practices of ancient healing traditions and the tools of modern medical science. This allows us more responsibility over our own physical, mental, and spiritual well-being. To an ever greater degree, we can hope to increase the span and improve the quality of our lives.

What is healing?

To begin with, it is important to understand two profound distinctions. They were beautifully expressed by a friend I deeply admire, Dr. Michael Lerner, founder of the Commonweal Cancer Support Program in California, during an interview with the American television journalist Bill Moyers. The first distinction is between curing and healing. "Curing," Michael says, "is what allopathic mainstream medicine has to offer, when it can, and that's what the physician brings to you. Healing is what you bring to the encounter. . . . Healing comes from inner resources." An example: the doctor sets a broken leg, but the knitting and restoration of the bone comes from an internal healing process.

"Another important distinction is that between disease and illness. The disease is defined biomedically. But the illness is the human experience of the disease. There is a similar distinction between pain, which is the physiological phenomenon, and suffering, which is the human experience of pain."

The Cancer Support Program allows people to explore conditions under which recovery can occur through stress reduction, health promotion, and group support. Yoga is a part of this program, and Michael describes it as "a useful package of effective stress-reduction practices such as gentle stretching exercises, deep-breathing exercises, meditation, and progressive deep relaxation." And then he adds: "But sometimes the language gets in the way. People hear 'Yoga,' and they think of some strange foreign practice . . . if the word gets in the way, it should be thrown out and replaced by some other package of ways of relaxing the mind and the body."

I agree, wholeheartedly and without reservation. I've taught stress-reduction programs for government leaders and health professionals in countries where I've not only been asked not to use the word "Yoga"—but also not even to mention the word "mind"! Also, techniques fostered by Krishnamacharya are now used in treatment programs for physically and mentally afflicted children and adults in Europe, Asia, and North

America, who may never be aware they are practicing Yoga.

At the same time, I cannot resist hoping that one day Yoga will be understood in its universal meaning, unbounded by cultural or religious associations. My father always believed Yoga to be India's greatest gift to the world—freely given and without strings.

Particularly as it relates to healing, Yoga must be changed and adapted to individual needs and to different settings and societies. At the same time, there are aspects of this tradition which must be preserved because they offer insights into the nature of healing, enduring wisdom that can help us in ever-changing circumstances. It was one of the challenges that preoccupied my father—what to preserve, what to adapt. Involved are fascinating questions of balance. The consequences are immeasurable.

We know that healing comes from within. And we also know that this inner power can be influenced, for better or worse, by other people and our surroundings. So, how do we reach and work with the source of healing?

The *Yoga Sutras* answer this question very directly: all healing comes from God. Does this mean that only the religious will heal? Obviously not. Please recall that Patanjali describes God as *Ishvara,* the Eternal Teacher: "the ultimate teacher . . . the source of guidance for all teachers: past, present, and future." From this, we begin to understand one of the contributions that Yoga makes to our understanding of healing and how it works. This is the relationship between a teacher and a student that leads to improved health, to that wholeness we recognize as the harmonious union of body, mind, and spirit.

Here, again, we encounter the commonplace. What could be more constant in our lives than the teacher-student relationship? It begins with our parents, continues with all variety of specialized instructors, and as adults takes us, perhaps sometimes unwittingly, into situations where we become teachers. This happens with our own children, with younger people, with those who seek to share our skills. There can be unforgettable teacher-student learning situations with people we briefly meet and never see again—as any foreigner who's ever encountered a New York taxi driver for the first time can attest! Everyone now reading this book is largely the product of a lifetime of teacher-student relationships. Commonplace relationships, yes, but responsible for almost all that allows us to be who we are, and who we might be.

We are talking about something more when we speak of the teacher as healer, as one who furthers recovery, growth, and wholeness in our lives. We expect this to be an individual possessed of special skills. And there must be something more.

For me, the perfect example of such a teacher is my father. What Krishnamacharya understood so well is that to treat an individual as a unique, whole entity is more than a matter of technique and talent. All possible knowledge of that individual's physical, mental, family, social, cultural, and religious circumstances must be brought to bear. Krishnamacharya was a physician, with all the necessary degrees and training in Ayurvedic medicine. He possessed enormous knowledge of nutrition, herbal medicine, the use of oils, and other remedies. All of his other studies, too, were brought to his work as a healer, including law, history, logic, religion, astrology, and so forth. Each of these might have been accompanied by a titles, such as "Doctor" or "guru" but he would only allow himself to be referred to as "Professor" — or as a "Yoga teacher." In fact, when he was very old I even heard him say, "How can I call myself a teacher, when I have so much to learn?"

My father also was well aware that his skills as a healer were mainly what attracted people to his teachings about Yoga, beginning with the Maharaja of Mysore. After arriving in Chennai, it was as a healer that most people sought Krishnamacharya out—many sent by (and including) physicians. Regardless of how sick they were or what manner of treatment he might prescribe, none were patients. They were always students meeting with their teacher.

The question of what it is to be a teacher and a student in a healing relationship was central to my years of study with Krishnamacharya. It was the theme that ran through all of our lessons on *asana, pranayama,* chanting, scriptures, and so much more. I also had had the advantage from early childhood of watching him at work. Some of those memories are so vivid.

I remember neighbors in Mysore, a married couple who could not have children, who came to our home. My father interviewed and examined them, gave them advice about diet, and recommended certain exercises. Then, unseen by the couple, he took ashes from the fireplace where my mother warmed our bath water; wrapped the ashes in a piece of folded newspaper, and gave the packet to the man and wife. It was their special medicine. A few months later, they came again, delighted, because the wife was pregnant—and later gave birth to a healthy child.

This business with the ashes in newspaper happened more than once, always successfully, with other infertile couples. Reflecting in later life, it made no sense to me until I connected it with another memory. Despite the long hours he worked in Mysore, from before dawn to late at night, my father always made up his own prescriptions, even if they were quite common. My mother would ask, "Why don't you just send them to an apothecary?" And my father would reply: "No, it's important that they get them from me."

I know that this sounds peculiar: what some Westerners might call a placebo effect, meaning only that the cure took place but cannot be explained. Whatever intrinsic value that packet of ashes possessed one cannot imagine. But it was a focal point in the broader nature of the ability of the healer to inspire confidence. My father's great learning and his reputation, too, were part of his ability to give people faith that he could heal them. This is a universal aspect of the healing process. If we consult a famous surgeon, how much more confidence we have to see his or her walls covered with diplomas from famous medical schools, to hear of his or her fabulous surgical accomplishments—to receive a special prescription.

And so, in Yoga, we recognize the interaction of faith and devotion as the starting point, the foundation of the healing relationship. The student places his faith in the teacher, and the teacher devotes all of his skills, experience, and energy to the well-being of the student.

As a child I also learned as a matter of course the power of this bond of trust and devotion. My brothers and I were often called upon by my father to demonstrate *asanas* in his Yoga classes. There was one posture where I was required to mount a platform, sit cross-legged, and stretch backward arching my spine in as high an arc as possible. Then, my father would stand on my chest! I was a skinny, even frail child but it never occurred to me that if I did the posture as taught I could not support my father's entire weight. He would never do anything to hurt me. I don't recall feeling much weight at all.

Although it can be described simply, there is nothing simple about the healing relationship. Why is it that a skilled doctor with many degrees can give a prescription to a hospital patient and nothing happens? Then, a nurse with a warm, affectionate manner will give the same drug to the same patient who then begins to feel much better? Many physicians will, at some point, encounter this phenomenon, and there is no scientific explanation.

I must confess that my own first effort as a teacher was a disaster, almost fatal to my student! It was a dramatic lesson in the eternal truth that everything we do has consequences. It all began with what seemed like a harmless fib.

I was working as an engineer in Chennai, and one evening I had plans to go to the cinema with a group of friends. My boss walked in and told me that I'd have to work late that night. I really wanted to be with my friends, and so I said, "I'm sorry, sir, but I can't. I have two Yoga students coming for lessons with me this evening and I can't break the appointment."

"I didn't know you were a Yoga teacher," my boss said. "All right, you can go. But only on the condition that you will teach me Yoga, too." I went off and had a wonderful time with my friends.

A few days later, as we had agreed, my boss came to our home. I had decided that I would have him do a few easy exercises from the program that my father had taught me. So, I had the boss raise his arms over his head, breathing as I had been taught, and turning slightly. He did and suddenly collapsed to the floor. His breath stopped, the color in his face darkened, and there didn't seem to be any pulse. In a panic I ran for my father, who rushed back with me and began working over my boss, talking him back to consciousness and helping him to breathe. Soon, the poor man was fully recovered. He was a very fat man and in terrible physical condition. My father gently worked with him some more, showed him some different exercises, and the man left our home in fine spirits. Rather shamefaced, I later explained to my father all that had happened. "Why didn't you come to me?" he demanded. "You could have killed him!"

The experience taught me in the most unforgettable way the meaning of the primal universal law of all healing traditions, ancient and modern: "Do no harm!" It also awakened in me a new curiosity. How was it that, drawing upon my own knowledge of Yoga, I could teach a simple exercise with such terrible results? How was it that my father could begin with an unconscious student and not only bring him around but also continue with a lesson that made the man feel so much better than when he arrived?

Witnessing the progress of students of my father had awakened my interest in Yoga. The experience with my boss began the fascination with the nature of its teaching. From that moment on, studies with my father took on a new dimension in which I observed and tried to understand the ways in which he worked with students. Incidentally, my boss held no grudge. He became my first Yoga student—taught under Krishnamacharya's strict guidance.

Before describing how my father went about his calling, I must again emphasize that Yoga in the healing process is primarily used in chronic, or long-term situations. We don't deal with emergencies or traumas, nor with early onsets of disease such as fevers, cardiac attacks, or strokes. Yoga is a gradual process of recovery, maintenance, and improvement. It requires patience and discipline and no small amount of faith. That is the way it works. This is very difficult for some individuals to grasp, particularly Westerners who expect the kind of quick, dramatic results that scientific cures often produce. Also—and this can be very frustrating to some—we cannot guarantee any specific results because each individual situation is different from any other, each uniquely complex.

The people who came to see my father often had exhausted all other avenues of treatment. They were sometimes sent by their doctors, who would say, "You know, you have tried everything else. Why don't you go to Krishnamacharya? Maybe he can help you." People sought him out at the recommendation of friends or of his other students. Or they might have heard the tales of Krishnamacharya's legendary powers.

Even after he had agreed to meet with someone, my father might keep him or her waiting days or even weeks for an appointment. This was not uncaring. It was part of the emotional and mental preparation of the student for the encounter, and there was no emergency. The first meeting was very important. Krishnamacharya read people with the same uncanny penetration with which he read ancient texts. If he felt that someone was insincere or doubtful, he would send them away. This had nothing to do with vanity. He knew that he couldn't help such people—that they were wasting time, money, and possibly the opportunity to find help elsewhere. For any hope of a successful outcome, Krishnamacharya's student had to possess a willingness to trust, or at least an openness to guidance and new experience.

His examination of a student was very detailed. It also revealed much about the fundamental nature of the Yogic approach. Krishnamacharya was rather skeptical about Western medicine because he felt much of its knowledge was based upon dissection in anatomy labs. As he put it, "What can you learn from a dead body? What can breath do for a corpse?" His examinations strove to discover as much as possible what was happening in all the complex systems that make up a living individual.

What did Krishnamacharya look for in an examination?

In the broadest sense—and this is true of other Eastern healing traditions—he was looking for what had upset or hindered the harmonious union of body, mind, and spirit. The significant concept here is "harmonious union." No disease is localized. Although it may have a local system in which it operates, it will signal its occurrence throughout the conglomeration of physical and mental systems. The illness afflicts the totality. Also, no disease is an accident. Something caused it. My father would not have used these terms, but ready examples are genetic inheritance or the stress that leaves one vulnerable to illnesses ranging from a common cold to cancer, heart disease, and strokes.

Once again, I must apologize for only being able to sketch out Krishnamacharya's methods. After thirty years of study with him, I know there are still things he could do that no one else can.

The first stage was that the person seeking help had to be *there.* This is not as obvious as it sounds. Any health professional will tell you—and I have certainly experienced—the numbers of people who seek advice about treating ailments of friends or relatives. Such questions are unanswerable. The individual must be physically present.

Krishnamacharya would begin by getting an overall impression of the person: the color of the skin, the eyes; the quality of the voice and the breath; posture and body movement. He would ask in detail about his or her life, work, and family. He would go into the experience of the illness, its history and its effect.

While questioning an individual, my father would touch certain parts of the body to see if there was anything unusual, and he would take the pulse.

Reading the pulse is extremely important in our system—similar but not identical to the techniques of Chinese and Tibetan medicine. It involves the use of three fingers, each with a slightly different pressure, along the left and right wrists. This indicates the quality of the flow of *prana* through the *nadis,* those channels through which energy enters and moves through the body. The pulse can reveal enormous amounts of information about actual and even incipient conditions. By taking the pulse, Krishnamacharya often could tell if a woman was pregnant—even the sex of the unborn child.

It takes years of practice and experience to be able to read the pulse in this manner: the teacher must himself be very sensitive and prepare himself for each reading. The pulse may in addition be taken at other points of the body, such as the navel or ankles. And I must add that even the taking of the pulse might have a healing effect.

Not long ago, I was talking with a good friend who is also on the Board of Trustees of the Mandiram, Dr. B. Ramamurthi. He is one of the world's most respected neurosurgeons, one of the first physicians to perform brain surgery in modern India, and a senior member of medical societies in Asia, Europe, and North America. The subject of our conversation was the advantages and disadvantages of the marvelous technological instruments that, while greatly increasing the physician's capacity to diagnose, also put a kind of barrier between physician and patient. Dr. Ramamurthi, who does an enormous amount of charity work for the poor, laughed and told the story of an elderly woman from a rural village who came to see him. "I knew the moment she walked in it was a simple case. She had a neuralgic pain in her face. I said, 'Don't worry. I will give you some medicines and you will be all right.' She said, 'What, doctor? You have not touched my hand and seen! The touch of your hand will help me.' There is a term in Tamil which refers to the good hand or the healing hand. So, the doctor should touch the patient, make a physical contact, touch the forehead . . . reassure. With these things you are able to convey the energy of your confidence.

"That was twenty years ago," Dr. Ramamurthi continued. "I've never forgotten it. In India, many people believe in the power of the healer's touch, and we must not leave that out."

Nor can the touch, so far as the pulse is concerned, be left out of the beginning of the Yoga teacher's relationship with the student. It is a communication of what the student needs.

My father's examination might extend over two or three appointments. And at some point, he would ask: "Can you follow my guidance?" This was the moment when the student had to decide whether to place trust in Krishnamacharya. If he did, then the healing relationship began.

Drawing upon his great knowledge of Ayurveda, Krishnamacharya would in most cases prescribe a change in diet. Medicines would also be given. And he might insist upon certain changes in living habits, such as giving up a sport or changing the schedule of sleep.

As regards Yoga practice—*asana, pranayama,* and so forth—Krishnamacharya said that it can help in two directions. They are called *langhana,* or contraction, and *brmhana,* or expansion. These are fundamental concepts that run through all dimensions of Yoga. Postures that involve forward bending, or contracting, are *langhana,* while those that stretch or arc backwards are *brmhana.* Similarly, inhalation, which expands the lungs and abdomen are *brmhana;* exhalation, drawing the abdomen inward, is *langhana.*

In practice, we see such superficial examples as the overweight person who needs to cut down on salt and fatty foods, exercise more, including a program with forward bends, and focus on exhalation. This is movement in the *langhana* direction. The opposite, *brmhana,* takes the underweight individual toward more food, more inhalation, and, perhaps, more rest.

These concepts also pervade the nature of the teacher-student relationship. For instance, if the teacher is not very firm but speaks in a smooth, pleasant manner, even postures that are *brmhana* can become *langhana,* while a teacher shouting "RELAX! RELAX!" is certainly not engaging *langhana.*

Krishnamacharya did not originate these concepts, but he took them further than anyone I know as useful techniques for the modern world. Insomnia is a good example. It is not enough to teach a sedentary office worker to relax; they may need to be guided into more physical activity, or *brmhana,* to be followed by kinds of *langhana* practices that will ease them into slumber. People such as salesmen, engaged in excitable talk and movement all day, may be exhausted but too overwrought to rest, and should be taught lying postures with long, easy exhalations. We see the helpful application of these concepts in very serious conditions. Stroke victims, for example, may recover more slowly because impairments of movement and speech make them withdraw into themselves, fearful of exposing their limitations. Even very basic exercises and breaths that are *brmhana* appear to instill more confidence in their ability to re-occupy and participate in their surrounding life.

Krishnamacharya emphasized that such healing relationships must be on a one-to-one basis. Once he began working with a student, he would see him or her usually once a week to monitor progress and to change the program as needed. And to find out if the student was following his directions. He could tell at first glance if a student did not. My father was very strict about students following his advice, and even in his mellower old age he could terrify those who lapsed. This arose from his deep caring, his devotion to the student's welfare. With greatest respect to his memory and his genius, I think perhaps sometimes he was a little too strict. There was a successful businessman who suffered from diabetes, who loved to ride his horse each morning. My father told him he had to give up riding. The man tried because Krishnamacharya's teaching had helped him feel better and also to reduce the dosage level of his medication. But he could not give up his beloved horses. So he gave up Yoga! I learned of this only recently when he came to see me about some other problems.

The one-to-one relationship between teacher and student is essential not only for the suffering individual but, eventually, for any serious student of Yoga. This is because progress beyond a certain point requires the total concentration of teacher and student in the learning situation. There can be no distractions.

On the other hand, there is a definite role for group classes, often as complements to the individual teaching. We see this especially in cancer or cardiac support groups where the presence of others provides encouragement and understanding. Also, most people are introduced to, and undertake the earlier phases of their Yogic studies in classes.

I used to watch my father in classroom situations with the keenest interest, partly to study his technique but also to marvel at his powers of observation. Often, he would sit in a chair and read a newspaper while giving *asana* practice. And yet he could make the most minute correction or change in the way a student performed a posture or controlled the breath. My mother used to say that Krishnamacharya never saw with his eyes open, but with them closed. His perceptions went into a person, deeper than any simple matter of whether the head turned in a certain way or a knee was straight. I can only suggest his depth of perception through an example.

An American friend of mine wanted to have my father look at his astrological chart, so I asked him to have it written in Tamil. I showed it to my father and he said, "I don't want this. I want to see the fellow."

I presented the young man and my father looked at him and said, "He cannot be a Leo, his chart is wrong. He can only be a Pisces." Later, when we were alone, my friend was very annoyed. He said, "How can my birth date be wrong? Your father is a nut!"

"Look, you asked for this." I said. "Maybe you had better ask your mother."

He sent a cable to his mother, who replied, "I don't care what your astrologer says, that is the right date." But my friend pursued the question, and checked out the medical records. I won't try to guess what was behind the error, but the records proved that his presumed birth date was wrong and my father was right. That is only one example of Krishnamacharya's powers of observation, and neither I nor anyone else ever fully comprehended them.

Astrology, by the way, was a subject in which I had absolutely no interest. My father didn't mind as long as I was studying with him as a student. He taught me what I wanted to learn as I wanted to learn it, including, at first, no mention of God or prayers or anything religious. This changed when I began teaching. Then, the focus shifted to what my students might need, and so he insisted that I should get a reasonable acquaintance with astrology. In India, astrology is intrinsic to our lives, determining marriages, important decisions—even the date of elections! A surprising number of Westerners, I've discovered, are not only interested in our astrology but also base their actions in terms of auspicious or inauspicious dates on the calendar. It is the teacher's duty to adapt to the student's needs. For myself, I never looked at the chart my father drew up at my birth. And Krishnamacharya's attitude was summed up in this way: "Anyone who truly loves and worships God doesn't need astrology."

Studying with my father had a consequence he had not expected, and which dismayed him. I decided to give up engineering and devote my life to being a teacher of Yoga. I was a fairly good engineer but my heart wasn't in it. Yoga drew all my curiosity, opening up boundless possibilities of change and discovery both for myself and others. It was a journey, an adventure without end.

"But you're an engineer!" My father protested. "You have a good income, you have status. If you become a Yoga teacher you'll always be poor. You won't be able to marry and provide for your children." Knowing how much I enjoyed my social life, he added, "You'll lose all your friends!"

He was speaking, of course, from the experience of terrible hardship in his own early years, and it was true that Yoga teachers had no social status whatsoever in our rapidly modernizing India. But my mind was made up, and my father reluctantly went along. As a man who cherished personal independence, he acknowledged it in his sons to a degree unusual in our culture.

And so, Krishnamacharya began the process of teaching me to be a teacher. Once he accepted my choice, he could not have been more generous and supportive. Still, a few years after my decision, when it came time to meet the family of my future wife, my father told me: "Under no circumstances tell them you're a Yoga teacher!"

As it turned out, I never suffered any of the difficulties that my father and uncle underwent in the early years of their teaching. I continued to earn money as an engineering consultant, and started acquiring a few students. What success I achieved early on was due in no small part to one of the greatest teachers—one of the greatest intellects—of the twentieth century: Jiddu Krishnamurthi. Krishnaji not only gave my career a boost. By his example, he also taught me what it was to be a student.

There are many books by and about Krishnamurthi. His story is so rich and complex that I can give only a few highlights for those unfamiliar with him. He was born to a poor family and was discovered just after the turn of the century, on a beach near Chennai, by Annie Besant, head of the Theosophical Society. The society was dedicated to universal brotherhood; the study of comparative religion, philosophy, and science, and the investigation of "unexplained laws of Nature and the powers latent in man." Then as now, the society's worldwide headquarters were in Chennai, in beautiful parklands bordered by the Adyar River and the Bay of Bengal. Annie Besant remains one of the most beloved figures in India for her early championship of independence and also for her devotion to the education of the poor and of women.

The Theosophical Society had a membership that included many wealthy and powerful individuals in America and Europe, and their destiny, they felt, was to prepare the way for the new "Messiah," the great world teacher. In 1909, when she first laid eyes on the fourteen-year-old Krishnamurthi, Mrs. Besant believed that the divinely promised teacher had arrived.

Krishnamurthi was carefully trained and educated in India and Europe. And then, at the age of thirty-four, in a celebrated address he renounced all such claims. Krishnamurthi disbanded his followers, informed them that there was no such thing as a guru, and that each individual must find his or her own way to truth. To give some indication of Krishnaji's way of thinking, here are a few of the remarks he made at that address in 1929:

> I maintain that truth is a pathless land, and you cannot approach it by any path whatsoever, by any religion, by any sect. . . . Truth being limitless, unconditioned, unapproachable by any path whatsoever, cannot be organized; nor should any organization be formed to lead or to coerce people along any particular path. If you understand that, then you will understand how impossible it is to organize a belief. A belief is a purely personal matter, and you cannot and must not organize it. If you do, it becomes dead, crystallized; it becomes a creed, a sect, a religion, to be imposed on others. This is what everyone throughout the world is attempting to do. Truth is narrowed down and made a plaything for those who are weak, for those who are only momentarily discontented. Truth cannot be brought down, rather the individual must make the effort to ascend to it. You cannot bring the mountaintop to the valley. If you would attain to the mountaintop you must pass through the valley, climb the steeps, unafraid of the dangerous

> precipices. You must climb upwards to truth . . . I maintain that no organization can lead man to spirituality. . . . The moment you follow someone you cease to follow truth. . . . I am concerning myself with only one essential thing: to set man free.

After the address, Krishnamurthi went his own way. The rest of his life was devoted to travel and lecturing, talking eventually to hundreds of thousands of people, and gaining renown among several generations of the world's finest minds as the "intellectual's philosopher."

I knew none of this when, in 1965, Krishnamurthi paid one of his regular visits to Chennai and asked to meet my father. It turned out that he lived nearby, and he was waiting eagerly at the door to receive us. He asked to see how we practiced *asana*, and under my father's direction my brother and I gave a twenty-minute demonstration. "I want to study with you," Krishnamurthi said, and my father replied: "We'll think about it." The next day, Krishnamurthi's secretary came to our small flat and asked when the study might begin. My father said, "My son will teach him." And chose me.

It was a rather awkward situation. For one thing, Krishnaji had been studying Yoga for years with my uncle, and he was already well-versed in practicing *asana*. I had only been studying seriously with my father for a few years. Also, at our first meeting I was only twenty-seven years old and he was a world-famous figure nearing seventy. He had been studying Yoga longer than I had been alive!

On the first day he set the tone of our relationship, as student to teacher, which never changed. He greeted me at the door, ushered me into the room. He would never sit before I did, nor allow me to arrange the carpet upon which he did his exercises. His was an attitude of total respect.

I asked to see his exercises and he performed a number of highly advanced *asanas*, including the headstand, shoulderstand, hand balances, and many difficult back arches. His chest and neck were tight, the breath restricted, and occasional tears filled his eyes. Yet he was enthusiastic. We talked about the need to reduce these symptoms and about his health, which was delicate. Later, my father and I discussed the situation in detail, and he devised an entirely different program. The difficult postures were to be eliminated. In place of the shoulderstand, Krishnaji was to lie on his back with legs raised against a wall, which we later changed to legs bent at the knees over a stool. No more headstand. A very easy head movement eased the neck stiffness. Some of these movements were absolutely new to me. My father had adapted underlying principles of Yoga to the specific problems, not merely drawn upon a traditional repertoire.

At our next meeting, I said to Krishnaji: "Sir, you must stop all that you are doing and I will instruct what my father has asked me to teach you."

"Sir," he said, "I will follow whatever your father teaches." It was amazing. Imagine if someone tells you that something you have been doing for years—it could be anything: pruning plants, sewing, carpentry—is all wrong and you must change. I know if someone said it to me about Vedic chanting, I'd probably revolt. With Krishnamurthi, every single technical detail that I taught was completely different from what he had known before. In two days, there was no trace of his previous Yoga.

Krishnamurthi's health began to improve, and not long after he invited me to join him in Switzerland to continue his lessons and teach some of his friends. My father said, "He is a world teacher. You must go." Still, I was reluctant because of Krishnaji's long association with my uncle, for whom I have always felt respect and affection. It was only after Iyengar wrote and gave me his blessing that I felt free to accept the invitation. This was a big event. As my father had predicted, I had lost most of my friends when I switched from engineering to Yoga. Being invited to Europe suddenly revived my "status," and my old friends came with garlands to the airport to see me off.

In Switzerland, Krishnaji was attentive and caring. He taught me Western table manners, and saw that I was comfortable and had delicious meals. He often wrote reassuring my parents that I was being well-looked after, noting, "We are all strict vegetarians." We met each day, sometimes more than once, and he approached each lesson in a spirit of humility, respect, and enthusiasm. I only attended one of his talks, and he never suggested that I learn anything about his ideas. What Krishnaji taught by the word, I don't pretend to know. But he taught me so much by his example: punctuality; cleanliness (everything was immaculate in his rooms); dignity of labor (he always cleaned his own bathroom so that it would be as clean as the servants or chambermaids had left it); respect for others; humility before the teacher whatever his age or status; willingness to learn thoroughly, and a respect for all cultures. His only advice to me was: "Sir, don't become a guru, don't exploit, don't become rich."

Our relationship continued until near his death in 1986. We would usually meet once or twice a year, either in Europe or Chennai. Because of my father's great age, Krishnaji had told him: "Sir, your knowledge must not be lost. You must teach your son everything." He even offered to finance these studies so that I wouldn't be distracted. It was a generous offer because his own organization was financially hard-pressed at the time. While appreciating his intent, I refused. Krishnaji's interest and support had other consequences. Studies with my father took on even more depth and, as time passed, a sense of urgency. Also, I began teaching students from Europe and America, as well as growing numbers in India.

During the next few years, I married and began a family. The marriage was arranged, a custom Westerners have discarded. For me and my family there was no question that Menaka would be my ideal life's companion. My father didn't even bother to cast her horoscope. She was a young girl, with little education, from a poor family. Soon after we were married, I asked what I might give her. "I want a house," she said, "and then I will be content." We found a large, comfortable home, my parents moved in with us, and we settled down to family life. Menaka is more than a devoted wife and mother to our three children. Through constant study and deep caring, she has become one of the finest Yoga teachers. I say that not as her husband but as her teacher. These are very distinct relationships. My relationships with Krishnamacharya were those of father-son and teacher-student. Each of these ties can be filled with love and respect, but they are very different.

As a student, I would approach my father each day and sit in his presence. We would begin with prayer, and then he would spend two or more hours on *asana* and *pranayama.* We would turn to texts that he had asked me to study, ensuring first that I had committed them to memory. I would then bring up questions that I had. These might be about our studies, and would also include questions that had arisen in my teaching. This was of incalculable benefit for both me and my students. During all those years, whether they ever met him or not, they were blessed with an immediate link to Krishnamacharya's vast wisdom and experience.

Our household rhythms had a different character, and my father's never changed until the last few years of his life. In his nineties, a typical day began at two A.M. when he awakened, prepared his tea, and performed two or three hours of *asana,* including difficult variations of the headstand, and *pranayama.* At five A.M. he began his *puja,* or worship, by hand-ringing a heavy bronze bell that produces a loud, resonant "OM." The ringing went on for several minutes, which awakened the whole household—not without some grumbling.

At 6:30 A.M., Krishnamacharya prepared his breakfast, and exactly at seven I arrived for the first of what might be several lessons during the day. At eight, he received his own students. Whenever Krishnamacharya wanted to go out, usually to buy his own food at the market, he would hire his own rickshaw driver. He would never let me take him in the car.

It offended his sense of independence. He was on friendly terms with all the drivers who pedal these small carriages, and with the food sellers. His greatest joy was teaching and playing with children, especially his grandchildren. Krishnamacharya always had sweets at hand for himself and children. Even today, I meet middle-aged people who remember the almond powder he'd given them as children at the end of a lesson. Very late in life my father developed an interest in cricket because his grandchildren were mad for it.

I won't pretend there weren't moments of friction: what healthy family doesn't have them? My father was scrupulous about observing every ritual—and we Indians have so many of them!—in every last detail. We had the thread ceremony for my children, their formal entry into Brahminism, which in most houses takes about fifteen minutes. In ours, it took three days and I lost all patience because it went on so long.

Perhaps the most powerful impression of my father as a teacher is that the more I studied with him, the more amazed I grew at what seemed to be his limitless knowledge. Indian priests would come to chant with him, sometimes for hours, and I began to realize that they didn't know how to chant. They changed completely in my father's presence. There were scholars who came from all parts of India—and he would speak with each in his own language, and teach them new things about their own traditions and philosophy, which they might have studied for most of their lives. There were also government leaders and politicians who sought him out both for healing and for guidance.

There came to our home, where I taught as well, a growing number of students who themselves wanted to be teachers. These included more and more foreigners, and also a very significant group of brilliant young students from the University of Madras.

They were attracted to Yoga not for health reasons, but because they wanted to explore its possibilities in improving their intellectual capacities.

They began to share Yogic techniques with other students at the university. My father particularly enjoyed this group. He would draw them into arguments about logic, and entrap them in one fallacy after another. "You're all eunuchs," he would laugh. "None of you can keep up with a true logician."

Our house was overflowing with family, students, and emerging teachers. It was because of the crowding more than any plan that the Mandiram was started. Halfway down the street I rented a large house with space for offices, individual classrooms, and one large lecture hall with a thatched roof on the top floor. My father permitted us the use of his name, gave his blessings, and occasionally taught classes or lectured. There was a very clear understanding between us, however, that this was my undertaking, my responsibility. The Krishnamacharya Yoga Mandiram was formally inaugurated in 1976.

Since its opening, more than twenty thousand people have come to the Mandiram. Among them are to be found every degree of physical and mental suffering; of spiritual longing, and of deep-felt curiosity. There are individuals on the brink of death with cancer, cardiac, or other terminal conditions. And there are some distraught because they feel sluggish in the morning. There are people desperately trying to recover health or physical functions after a serious illness and also champion athletes troubled by their failure to win in final playoffs. We see individuals dismissed elsewhere as "hypochondriacs" (as if that weren't in itself a form of suffering!) and others engaged in a lifelong quest to understand the soul.

More than twenty thousand people and more than twenty thousand entirely different situations—but each asks, in one form or another, "Can you help me?" And all we can answer, the only absolute guarantee each teacher can make is: "I can care."

That this answer leaves many intellectually unsatisfied, especially those who would like detailed cause-and-effect explanations, I can well understand. I am sorry about that. I can wish it were otherwise, but in truth I doubt if there will ever be a thoroughly satisfactory explanation of how Yoga works in any scientific, mechanistic sense.

From my own scientific training, I can go on at length about the biomechanics of *asana*—and there are countless articles on the subject. In the end such inquiries, though interesting, don't tell us very much. To give just two examples:

There is a belief that part of the efficacy of the shoulderstand is that it works upon the thyroid gland in the neck region. But that is also the region where the vagus nerve originates. Who is to say whether it is the thyroid or vagus nerve or something else being affected—and whether in sequence or simultaneously? You may also read that a benefit of the headstand is that it allows more blood to flow into the brain. But the neuroscientist Dr. Ramamurthi will point out that in reasonably healthy people, the brain protects itself. When a head-down posture, due to gravity, sends more blood flowing toward the brain, blood vessels in the brain immediately contract to ensure that the organ receives no more than the blood supply needed at that particular moment.

I don't wish to suggest that we may not in the future understand far more about how Yoga works. It's just that the scientific methods haven't yet revealed much. European scientists in the 1930s verified that my father could stop his breath and heartbeat for several minutes—but not how he did it.

We may be aided in our inquiries by newer approaches less dependent upon cause-and-effect sequence, for example by non-invasive brain-scanning techniques, or by new ways of thinking, such as chaos theory. In the meantime, we have undertaken research at the Mandiram under the direction of Dr. Latha Sathish, a Yoga teacher who is also a member of the psychology faculty at the University of Madras. In the context of her scientific background, Dr. Latha was operating under severe constraints.

First, we could not allow use of the double-blind method. This is a basic tool of research, dividing subjects into two groups: one receiving the proposed treatment, the other given a placebo or no treatment at all. Our first study involved asthma patients. We know from long experience that Yoga will help, sometimes very considerably, in about two-thirds of such cases. By definition, a double-blind study would deny help and improvement to one-third of those involved. That would be unconscionable.

Dr. Latha created a program that involved individual cases studied over a period of five years, which has expanded to ten. Obviously, the samples are small—an anecdotal approach rather than the preferred statistical analysis of Western research.

As we continued to explore and develop a research paradigm, we lost another element of traditional methodology. We had to throw out the hypothesis—that reasoned proposition against which all observations and results are tested. By its nature, a hypothesis is an expectation within a defined paradigm. There are no standard solutions, no standard problems, and a host of individual circumstances that affect any outcome. These include the student's trust and discipline, family support, school or working conditions, to name only a few. Ultimately, we discarded the word "paradigm" from our research vocabulary as well.

Dr. Latha's detailed case studies do reveal some patterns; perhaps it is better to call them *likelihoods*. Individuals who've suffered from asthma for about five years or less seem more susceptible to improvement than those who have lived with the disease for longer periods. Improvement in this instance can mean anything from complete cessation of symptoms to a reduction in medication. Individuals with high blood pressure are more likely to show improvement than those whose condition is accompanied by headaches. In some students, there is a noticeable decline in the frequency and severity of migraines. Under carefully supervised teaching, women report a more comfortable pregnancy and easier childbirth. Why any of these results occurs, we cannot say—all the more so because most of these students are also under a physician's care. All that a teacher of

Yoga can guarantee, to repeat, is: "I can care." It appears that more often than not something beneficial will happen.

I've been describing attempts to understand how Yoga works from the scientific perspective. More is to be learned when we revert to the integrity of Yoga in its own terms—the Yoga of Patanjali as taught by Krishnamacharya.

In the previous chapter I offered a brief description of *agni,* the "fire" located in the *chakra* above the navel, as well as *apanas,* the impurities that collect in the lower abdomen. In this formulation, the purpose of an inverted posture is to direct "fire," which burns upward, to cleanse impurities in the lower body. There are certain books and teachers who seem to suggest that a headstand or shoulderstand is the epitome of Yogic practice—something that a serious student must master. In fact, there are any number of spinal or back problems that rule out such postures. This is why my father changed Krishnamurthi's practice to more gentle ways of raising the legs to use the benefits of *agni* without the negative effects that he would have suffered from a headstand.

That is a specific example. For a deeper sense of how Yoga works in healing, Patanjali's original definition is the key: "Yoga is the ability to direct the mind exclusively toward an object and sustain that direction without any distraction." As we have seen, the first two stages involved are the ability to direct our minds, *dharana,* and the ability to develop interactions with what we seek to understand, *dhyana.* Combined, we may think of these two stages as the beginning of a process of "linkage."

Yoga always concerns the mind, and the mind is always attaching itself to something—an external object, a sensory experience, a mood, a thought. For better or worse, these attachments may be fleeting, jumbled, and onrushing, or they may be sustained, even obsessive. In part, it is by changing such attachments, by a progression of unlinking and relinking, that we may alter the mind's experience of suffering and illness.

Such changes are very much a part of cancer therapy. I remember the pain and suffering my mother experienced when she fell ill with lymphoma. Her experience taught me many things. She had all the characteristic sufferings of cancer, along with bouts of fever, malaria, and typhoid. Her weakened system developed a resistance to medicines and chemotherapy, and ultimately she underwent radiation treatments. There was a day when a new medicine completely disoriented her personality—only one day and then she was back to herself. She would take an autorickshaw for shopping or doctor's appointments, continued to cook for my father, and followed her own routine with poise and calm. The cancer could consume her body but she would not let it touch her mind. Her sister in Bangalore died of cancer and she was happy right up to the end. She never knew she had cancer!

Because modern science has made such progress, because so many malignancies can be treated and cured, the very word "cancer" is often more dreadful than the actual disease. It is the meaning and its effect on the mind that can intensify the illness. The meanings that link mind and disease heighten suffering with even relatively minor problems such as pimples, a small scar, constipation, or a toothache.

It is in changing this linkage that the role of the teacher is crucial. Once the mind is totally caught up in something, it is very difficult for us to begin the changes on our own. A student of Menaka's gives some indication of the process involved.

The woman was highly educated, a doctor, whose husband had gone to America. When she followed, she learned that her husband was divorcing her. She was also experiencing professional difficulties. By the time her physician suggested the Mandiram, the woman was in a serious depression, with headaches and insomnia, and had attempted suicide. There is considerable risk in dealing with someone whose balance is so fragile, especially for someone like my wife, who cares so deeply. Because she cared so much, though, Menaka was able to reach the woman and guide her toward the first postures and breathing exercises of Yogic practice. At first, these involved lying postures coordinated with breath, and a few twists and bends. This is helpful in situating the student in the present, momentarily detached from painful, gathered memories. While learning the skills associated with smooth movement and breath, the teacher imparted thoughts and feelings of warmth, energy, and growth. Exhalation was associated with relaxation thoughts, lightness, and the shedding of negative feelings. All we can say about why this is helpful is that despair slowly gives way to a sense of control. This control may begin with the slightest movement and counting during respiration. Even this links the mind, if briefly at first, to something new. As months went by, Menaka guided her student through stages of *asanas* and *pranayama* and cognitive linkages. In a letter, the student later remarked: "Skepticism and faith mingled in a strange mixture in my mind as I began my first session with my teacher. Yoga regulated my breathing first and gradually I gained a measure of control over my non-existent appetite, chaotic emotions, and threatening depression . . . my health and mental state have improved slowly but steadily."

Throughout the process, Menaka kept the woman safe in the knowledge that her teacher was always there for her, would answer the telephone at any hour. What cannot be ignored is that Menaka was the teacher that this student needed. Another teacher might have followed exactly the same approach with little or no results.

The use of Yoga in treating the mentally ill is being tested and incorporated elsewhere in India. It is part of a comprehensive program aimed at the rural poor about 350 miles south of Chennai, on the outskirts of the great temple city of Madurai. Here, Dr. R. Ramasubramaniam, a psychiatrist, and his European-trained wife created the Shrsti ("Creation") Foundation, which includes a pioneering residential program. Financial and other resources to help the mentally ill are scanty in most parts of the world. Dr. Ramasubramaniam has looked for ways that both effectively treat the patient and reduce the need for prohibitively expensive drugs. His findings include the fact that Yoga in combination with anti-depressants such as Prozac both accelerate patient improvement and decrease the dosage requirements. It also seems helpful in promoting quicker adaptation and skills for art, recreational, occupational and other therapies.

Mental illness, as the name implies, is an affliction besetting an individual that can lead to recovery from, or management of the condition. One of the greatest challenges we've confronted has been working with the mentally disabled, individuals physically deprived of full mental functions. This began in 1981, when a ten-year-old boy was brought to the Mandiram. He was overweight; his tongue protruded; he drooled. The boy's body would jerk about or stiffen every few minutes, and there were bouts of temper tantrums, crying, and destructive behavior. One of the boy's major problems was that he could not squat and kept soiling himself. We were asked to be part of an interdisciplinary team involved in setting specific goals for the boy's treatment. An orthopedic surgeon advised surgery to relax muscles so that the boy could squat, but we decided first to try a three-month program of *asanas* and other training.

I must admit that I was baffled. It is one thing to reach toward a mind afflicted with illness; quite another to deal with the mind of an individual whose brain is damaged in ways we cannot fully comprehend. I took the problem to Krishnamacharya, who was fascinated and challenged. As he considered the case, my father expressed that belief so intrinsic to his own greatness as a healer: "As long as there is breath, we can do something."

We devised a program and learned to our delight that the boy was an enthusiastic student. He exercised twice a day, and within a month he could squat well enough to use an Indian-style toilet, which, like the old-fashioned French version, is essentially a hole in the floor. His weight dropped, and his motor skills improved so that he could dine with his family and take part in other activities with children his own age. As these improvements occurred, the boy adapted more easily to other treatments and social situations, in part because of increased self-esteem.

We were brought into this case by Vijay Human Services (VHS), founded by Professor P. Jeyachandran, a clinical research psychologist with more than thirty years experience in the United States and India. It began a close association with VHS that has taught us valuable lessons about the true potential of all human beings, no matter what seem to be their inherent disabilities.

Regardless of the diagnosis—Down's syndrome, cerebral palsy, autism, or others—Dr. Jeyachandran and his colleagues are firm believers in early intervention. This led us to work with children at the early toddler stage, and this, in turn, led naturally to teaching mothers to be the Yoga teachers of their children. This not only helped the children, but also eased the terrible stress experienced by their mothers. We went on to discover the advantages of children teaching other children. My daughter and younger son became teachers in their early teens.

Even recently, there was a powerful new lesson. Our special children and their mothers arrived at the Mandiram, and it was such a beautiful day we decided to hold class in the garden. The children ran around at first, playing and picking fruit. Then, we observed that they calmed down more quickly than usual, and brought far more concentration to the movements, breath, and sounds that are part of their study. The beauty of the surroundings enhanced the healing process. Now, except on rainy days, all their Mandiram classes are held in the garden.

From the beginning of the Mandiram, it was evident that Krishnamacharya's knowledge of healing would become a legacy for the future only if we created new generations of teachers. This has become a priority. I devised a two-year diploma course for teachers of Yoga. Because my father had placed so much trust in me, and in the Mandiram, I made the course work very difficult. Experience and experiment have led to changes in the study program. What continually amazes me is the range of people who commit themselves to it. They have included business leaders, academics, economists, housewives, lawyers, health professionals—and an airline pilot and a customs official. All are motivated by a desire to learn more about Yoga; only a few will become teachers of Yoga. It is not the most brilliant intellect that makes such a teacher. It is the inner capacity to care about someone else more than yourself.

As the years passed, a few such teachers emerged. For my father, there was one more student to enter his life—Mala Srivatsan, a young woman of immense importance to the continuation of Krishnamacharya's work.

The member of a prominent family, Mala came to Krishnamacharya for treatment of severe asthma that she had suffered most of her life. She'd had the benefit of the finest medical treatment and an education in psychology. From the moment they met, Mala placed absolute trust in my father. She improved rapidly under his care. After a few months, Krishnamacharya did something I don't believe he'd ever done in his life. He asked her to continue as his student. This was totally unprecedented: always it was the student who sought the teacher.

I must admit that my mother and I were baffled by the fact that Mala came to see my father two or more times a week—even when he would see no one else. My father appreciated her value, though, and the last eight years of his life he introduced her to chanting and teachings previously forbidden to women. Later, Mala assumed position as Executive Trustee of the Mandiram.

Although he continued to see a few students, and his studies went on unabated, my father's final years were very difficult. At ninety-three he could still perform difficult *asanas*—including variations on the headstand many younger "masters" could not. When he was ninety-five, however, he fell and broke his hip. Because of the reputation of Krishnamacharya, several leading surgeons offered to operate—but he would have none of it.

Instead, he rigged up pulleys and ropes by his bed and began to experiment with new Yogic techniques for his own rehabilitation. Within two months he was able to walk, but the loss of full freedom of movement depressed him. "Now," he said, "I have lost my independence."

Worse was the loss of my mother, who died four years before he did. My father had the greatest respect for my mother. When we children would come home from school, he would always say, "Greet your mother first." There was a new closeness in their last years together, when they would sit and talk on the porch each evening. The days were past when she used me as a go-between with him for sensitive family matters. Krishnamacharya wept often and bitterly after she died—the only time I ever saw him cry—and I don't believe he ever got over it.

There is no avoiding suffering and death, which even the gods experience. No matter how much we try to hedge against it with our devotion to health and wisdom, death is inevitable. What is within our control is the experience of life itself. One of my favorite memories is the encounter between my father and a salesman who came one day to sell him insurance. Krishnamacharya listened for awhile, and then glared at the poor man. "Insurance!" my father thundered. "God is my insurance. Who are *you* to sell *me* insurance?" The salesman gathered his papers and fled.

In his ninety-eighth year, my father moved to a small house on the corner of the property. He wished to devote himself solely to worship, to *Narayana.* Not long after his next birthday, a young doctor whom be liked told him that he would die very soon, that the family must prepared. "Nonsense!" my father said. "I am not going to die now. It is not in my breath . . . and I know my breath."

It is one of the most remarkable things I'd ever heard him say. How many of us can say that we know our breath?

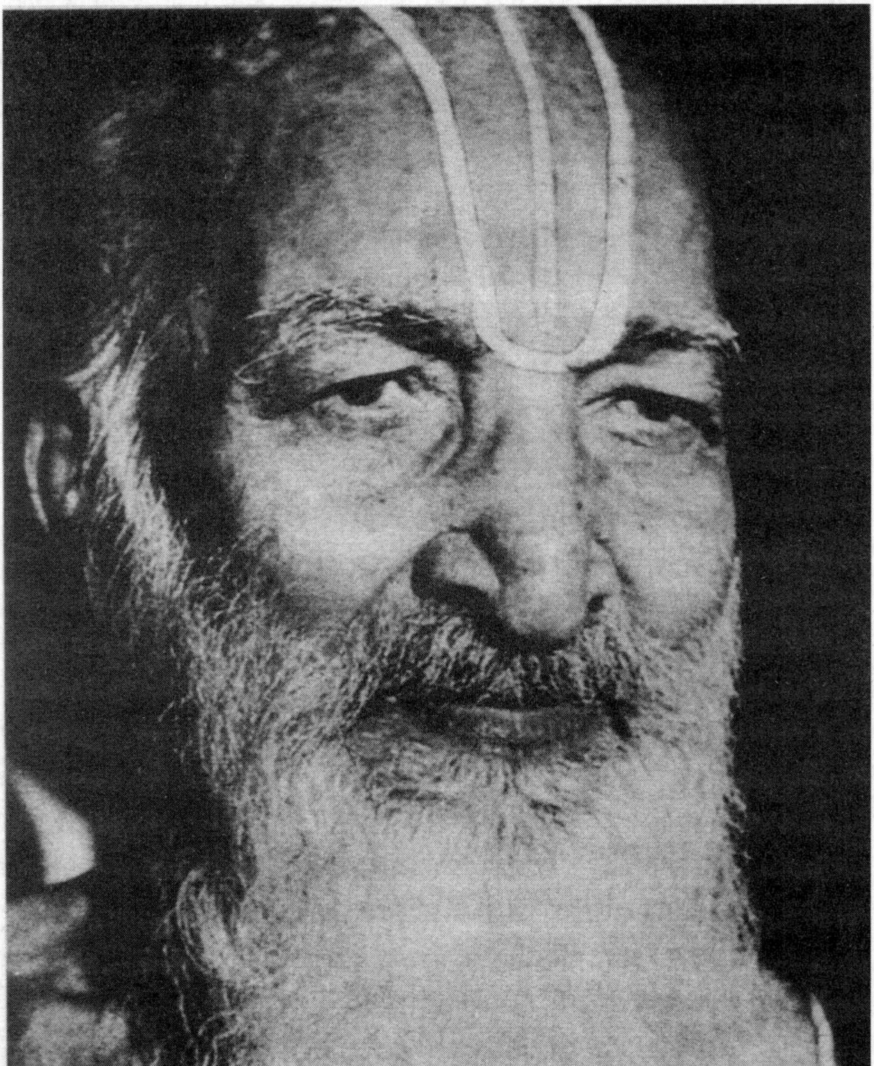

Krishnamacharya at His Centenary Celebration, Chennai, 1988

CHAPTER SEVEN

BEYOND THE KNOWN

Narayana . . . *this sacred name belongs to my tradition. You must find in your own culture the proper name to evoke, from your deep inner feeling.*

My father always said that the human life span is intended to be one hundred years. As his own one-hundredth birthday approached, there was a growing sense of excitement. It began within our family, but soon drew the attention of scholars, priests, public leaders, and especially students who had benefited from the teachings of Krishnamacharya. Six months before the actual date, which fell on November 18, 1988, an organizing committee was formed to plan a one-hundredth birthday celebration. Scores of people were involved in preparing a centenary tribute. There was one notable exception: my father announced that he would have absolutely nothing to do with it!

"Who am I to be honored?" he said. Krishnamacharya had moved out of our large house and into a small, two-room dwelling on the corner of the property. He now received very few visitors. Mala and I were the only students he saw regularly. He had entered that twilight of life when, in our tradition, one is granted the privilege of total devotion to

God. The duties of life, including work and raising a family, have been satisfied. In ancient times, individuals at this final stage were called *sannyasin,* and an elder would leave his past behind, go into the forest, and live as a wanderer begging food. This was considered to be the reward of a well-lived life, and the time for departure from it. It was, if I may mix traditions, like a return to Eden, an innocent return of the soul to God's creation. In our age, my father said, it was impossible to be a true *sannyasin,* so he went instead into as solitary a retirement as possible. He did not want the attention, the publicity, and above all the distraction from his worship entailed in any celebrations of his birthday.

On the other hand, it put the family in a rather awkward situation. The President and Prime Minister of India had both sent birthday salutations for the event. Well-wishers from abroad were to attend, including a crew of French filmmakers. The organizing committee had scheduled lectures and demonstrations relating to Yoga and Indian traditions. Commemorative publications were in the works. It was my chief task to ensure that we would have a guest of honor.

I wasn't very hopeful. During our years together, my father had placed enormous trust in me. All the same, I recognized when his will was unshakable—as when he had refused to continue dictating his autobiography or to teach me how to stop the heartbeat. This seemed to be one of those times. I tried with little success to convince him that the event was not to honor him, but that he would be honoring all those who attended. Then, I suggested that the centenary could be conducted as an act of worship. All who gathered could be brought into a festival of devotion and prayer. This aroused my father's interest. While he would not commit to attend, he agreed to instruct us how to proceed in paying homage to Vishnu, manifestation of the supreme God.

His first instruction was that people of all faiths should be welcome to participate. He insisted that the religious rituals be placed under the direction of a disciple of Shankaracharya. Further, Krishnamacharya directed that our own family priest should place himself under the direction of the Shankaracharya's representative. At this, the family priest was outraged: he stormed out of our house and hasn't returned to this day.

Lectures, seminars, and demonstrations took place in the weeks leading up to the centenary celebration. Three individuals received diplomas from the Mandiram's course for teachers. My children, who deeply loved their grandfather, were part of the event, my daughter, Mekala, performing on Krishnamacharya's ancient *veena*.

The celebration itself was a five-day festival, held in a great hall for worship built by the Shankaracharya and loaned to us with his blessings. On the peak day, my father's actual birthday, an act of devotion occurred which was, in the truest sense of the word, extraordinary. As specified by my father, there were 108 priests continuously chanting, and with them 108 bronze vessels, filled with water and placed in a precise design. One hundred and eight is a number that is sacred to us. Eight represents Sanskrit letters of the most important mantra: "OM na-mo-na-ra-ya-na-ya," which means: "All is of God. Nothing is by me, nothing for me."

With the recitations, there was a constant burning of incense and the offering of rice and sweetmeats, which is consumed in a deep firepit called a *homam*. This sacrifice is said to please the God, who holds a disk in his right hand that is the destroyer of evil. In his left, there is a conch shell that gives forth the holiest devotional chant, the sacred mantra, *OM*, which is learning and wisdom. Vishnu's mace and sword, too, are symbols of his power to protect mankind and nourish goodness. The chanting embraced not only the names of God, but also his revealed wisdom—verses from the *Mahabharata* and *Ramayana,* as well as many other Vedic texts and scriptures.

In addition to the hundreds of priests, dignitaries, and guests in the hall, there were also many hundreds waiting in a queue outside to receive my father's blessing. In India, it is a unique privilege to be blessed by a great man who has lived a hundred years. We had a special chair ready for my father, but right up to the beginning of the final day I wasn't sure that he would attend. He did arrive, however, and with the greatest humility acknowledged those present. Late in the evening the celebration neared conclusion, and someone asked Krishnamacharya to say a a few words. In the silence that followed, my father opened his mouth and issued the holiest mantra: "OM. . . ." The sound filled the entire hall. Some people say it went on for more than a minute. From my own years of counting movement of the breath I know that it went on for thirty to forty seconds. It was my father's only response, and an amazing one if you think about it: a man of one hundred years who can express such a prolonged sound upon a single breath.

Afterwords, my father instructed me to go to Kanchipuram and express his respect and gratitude to the Shankaracharya, which is what I did. Then, my father said, "Now, the only thing left for me is to teach you whatever I know. And you had better learn because I don't know how long I am going to last."

When I think back to Krishnamacharya's centenary, I realize that he had, at last, given us his true autobiography. It was not an account based upon names, dates, and places, nor about achievements, reputation, and honors. It was instead an evocation of his lifelong quest for learning, for service, and for devotion—a journey of mind and spirit. It was an uncanny experience to hear so many voices chanting so many sacred words, hymns, and scriptures; to witness expressions of the many facets of Yoga; and, above all, to take part in the rich, complex ritual worship of God. These were the unbroken strands, the design that made up the fabric of my father's life. In those few days, Krishnamacharya brought together so much of what he offered for the benefit of mankind and the journey of the soul.

Previously in this book, I have written of the teachings of Patanjali concerning the eight *angas,* or components, of Yoga. These are: *yama* (our attitudes toward others and our environment), *niyama* (our attitudes toward the self), *asana* (the practice of body exercises), *pranayama* (the practice of breathing exercises), *pratyahara* (the restraint of our senses), *dharana* (the ability to direct our minds), *dhyana* (the ability to develop interactions with what we seek to understand), and *samadhi* (complete integration with the object to be understood).

Always, we are working with mind and body—always moving toward a place we have never been or understood before; always moving in a direction beyond anything we have ever imagined possible; always moving toward unbounded, limitless truth and the ultimate union with God.

In my father's tradition, this is not a movement away from the worldly. It is movement toward the perfect experience of life for ourselves and others. This is the purest spiritual impulse, whether experienced by the individual or embodied in the essence of the great religions and their teachings.

From the practical perspective of Yoga, the first four components that lead to such movement are more or less subject to our control, given proper guidance, patience, and discipline. We can immediately begin to engage a change in our attitudes toward ourselves and others. This could be done as simply as introducing acts of courtesy where they have not existed in our behavior—for example, more kindly treatment, with a "thank you" and "please" when dealing with a waiter or other service person. By finding the right teacher or class, we can explore rudiments of *asana* and *pranayama.* But how do we go about the next series of change: Restraining the senses, acquiring the ability to choose and then link with an object?

My father taught that Yogic practice was to help make everything arise naturally. And there are practical means at our disposal to help achieve movement that leads to a richer linkage with life and with God. I'm referring to the universal practices of chanting, ritual, and meditation. We tend to think of them as esoteric when actually they are as instinctive as physical motion and the flow of breath. The truth of this, as is so often the case, can be witnessed in the actions of children and the surrounding events of everyday life.

Chanting can be heard in the singsong of small children as they go about their play. We chant at sporting events for a favorite team, at political rallies, and even in our self-exhortations when we quietly repeat to ourselves, "You can do it. You can do it." At work is the power of sound, perhaps to calm, perhaps to raise our emotional temperature.

In my father's teaching, this power has far greater potential. It can be used to heal the body, mind, and soul—and it can be an instrument in our efforts to change and to improve the quality of experience. There are chanting traditions found in diverse religions and cultures. For us, it is the chanting of the Vedas. While Vedic chanting is central to Hindu study and worship, it is essentially universal—like, for example, the *Yoga Sutras* or the *Bhagavad Gita*. There need be no confusion about this. My children fill our house with music from America and France, and this does not mean they have to be converted into Americans or French people. The power of Vedic chanting lies in the language, for Sanskrit has been called the great spiritual language of mankind. My father said it was the only complete language. With sixteen vowels and thirty-five consonants, Sanskrit offers infinite possibilities for producing and combining sounds, and this is further amplified in a very complex grammar. Each letter, each grammatical nuance can convey a vast range of meanings; and this, in turn, opens the language simultaneously to precision and to the subtle nuances that each individual brings to his or her interpretation and comprehension.

Vedic chanting is not singing. It is not, properly speaking, music at all. On the Indian musical scale there are seven primary notes; in chanting there are only three tones, with elisions upward and downward between them. The limitation is important because additional tones would distract from the meaning of the words and phrases, diminishing the power of the sound.

Chanting can only be learned from a teacher, and must be learned correctly, by heart, according to prescribed disciplines. Otherwise, so the ancient texts tell us, instead of conferring benefits the chants can do immense harm. To give a brief idea of chanting in practice:

It must be done in a clear voice, the loudness determined by the nature and duration of the chant. The cadence is determined by the need for fluid movement of sound and for clear understanding of the mantras. It is not only the placement of the tones, but also their relationship to one another that matters. Thus, the pitch is determined by the chanter's own vocal range, which often will expand—rising higher or lowering—over time.

I hope the reader will understand that there is no rule that requires any student of Yoga to study or master chanting. It is there as a possibility. If it works for you, do it; if not, don't.

In my case, my own mother tried to discourage me. I've never been musical and had a terrible voice. I began after a few years of study with my father, and my mother came to me and begged me to stop. "There is already to much noise in the neighborhood," she said. She had a point. In addition to the incessant sounds of crows, hawking peddlers, barking dogs, and jet airplanes roaring overhead, we then had one neighbor with a donkey that never stopped braying and another who was trying to learn the trombone. My mother most reasonably didn't want any additions to the din. With the greatest affection for her, I nevertheless refused. At first, the sounds were fretful but over the years of study I realized that in chanting I was gradually acquiring my father's voice, sounding more like him all the time. Chanting truly entered the rhythms of life, and my teaching.

It is fascinating to me, as a teacher, to observe when and how chanting may find a place in a student's practice. There are two very accomplished teachers of Yoga, Sonia Nelson and Martin Pierce, who've each studied with us for more than twenty years—and who both live in the eastern United States. Sonia was drawn to chanting almost instantly on her first visit to Chennai, and has adapted it into English with excellent results for her American students. Martin, perhaps because of an early discouraging experience with singing, choked up every time he attempted chanting during those two decades, and this certainly didn't prevent him from being a devoted, even inspired teacher of Yoga. Then, in the last couple of years, all the obstacles simply fell away and he embarked on an earnest, rapid study of the practice.

What are the benefits of chanting? The revered grammarian Panini mentions, among others, the protection and cleansing of sense organs, body, mind, and soul; the attainment of knowledge; lightness of body, and freedom from doubts. In our work, we see its benefits in such diverse areas as treatment for speech defects, helping with digestive problems, and reducing stress. It is very useful in teaching *pranayama* to children because they get bored with counting breaths, and in fact it seems that chanting helps with respiration in most individuals because it extends exhalation.

Beyond these immediately practical effects, there is the linking with the wisdom conveyed in the mantras. When I chanted with my father, I was bound to him and his teachings in a unique fashion, just as in his chanting he was once again linked to his own teacher—and so it stretches back through many centuries of teachers and students, the unbroken lineage of the *parampara*. In our tradition, when we chant we unite with God, who gave us the language, the practices of Yoga, and the wisdom of the Vedas. Even today, in India, if passersby hear the smallest beggar child chanting they will salute him and touch his feet. For in those moments, the child is the incarnation of God.

Rites and ceremonies—like a prescribed routine—are a series of actions that are repeated in a certain order. Children are quite ritualistic, as we often see when they are at play. And how upset a child can be if something interferes with the ritual of putting them to bed, preparing them for sleep!

Ritual is all around us. It marks major changes of status in our lives and occurs in social events ranging from organizational meetings to patriotic and national celebrations. The question becomes, how do we engage ritual that is best-suited to our private practice? Obviously, we can seek ritualistic experience in a church or temple, or in a great religious festival. Here, the question is whether we are a true participant, bringing freshness and enthusiasm to the occasion, or merely a witness. When the actions associated with ritual are mimicry or mechanical, it is like giving good ingredients to a bad cook—pure waste.

From culture to culture and religion to religion the varieties of ritual are endless. It should be noted, however, that in our ancient texts there is considerable emphasis upon the virtues of innovation and adaptation. This comes as a surprise to many who are considered experts, and also to those who believe that rituals are dead formulas from the past. In fact, ritual is meant to be filled with life and vitality.

Ritual is an aspect of *karma*—the things that I do, or have done, and their consequences. It is performed with the idea that we have something higher in our minds, not necessarily always God. The actions may be associated with daily activities; with events such as welcoming guests or undertaking a new project; with major transitions such as birth, marriage, and death; or with the cleansing of body and mind—for example, purification after we have transgressed some moral code. In formalized rituals handed down from the past, what occupies our minds is what occupied the minds of the ancients—again, a linkage with proven wisdom. As we connect in this way, we extend the limits of our understanding back through time. When we seek to discover or create rituals unique to our situation, we still must observe fundamental requirements. In every ritual, from the simplest to the most complex, there is:

- GEOMETRY: situating ourselves and the symbolic elements we employ—such as a candle, incense, or an object of meditation—in a certain relationship.
- STRUCTURE: the beginning, climax, and ending of the actions we perform.
- STRATEGY: the progressive sequence of action, thoughts, and prayers that lead to the fulfillment of the ritual.
- PURPOSE: the myriad possibilities of this karmic activity, which in Yogic practice is directed toward *dhyana.*

An example of a traditional ritual, sacred to Brahmins, is the *aradhanam,* or meeting with God. A businessman I know performs this frequently.

He enters the *puja* room in his home with a chalk mark on his forehead, a sign of his belief in Vishnu; a cloth around his waist indicating he is a servant of God, and the sacred thread of the initiated Brahmin wrapped around his torso circling his left shoulder. He uses his household gods in the form of wooden images of Rama and his consort, Sita; Laksmi, wife of Vishnu; and Rama's helper, the monkey god Hanuman. During the course of the ritual, he recites mantras from the Vedas, the Tamil Vedas, and the works of the great masters. During this period—and this is very important—he cannot touch or be touched by anyone.

As in any *dhyana,* this process of merging with God has distinct stages. He prostrates himself to God as a preliminary step to foster the proper mental attitude. After chants to awaken the sleeping gods, the devotee seats himself, observing the correct procedures for cleanliness, foundation, and posture. This is followed by the praise of God, during which the devotee recites various mantras and offers flowers, incense, and fruit to the deity, sanctifying them through prayer.

Having awakened God and praising him, the devotee then asks God to come to earth and sit with him, after which he welcomes God by ringing a special brass bell, each ring of which is the equivalent of saying *OM*. He offers God holy water. He burns holy oil. Now the devotee achieves the goal of *dhyana*—he is with God.

After this time with God, the devotee must return to the everyday world. He asks God to go back to sleep, and concludes the *puja* by prostrating himself and asking forgiveness for whatever mistakes he has made in his prayer.

Such a ritual takes place in the space of thirty to sixty minutes, and I once asked this gentleman how he finds time for it in the midst of his heavy responsibilities, including a high-pressure job and the demands of family. He answered: "It keeps me sane!"

In exploring the possibilities for designing ritual that leads to meditation, we adapt basic elements to the individual and his religious and cultural background. We have a student, who teaches Yoga in the Catalan region of Spain, for whom the essential symbol is her treasured twelfth-century cross with an image of Jesus. It is very rare because the image is smiling. For this young woman, it was important that Jesus should wear a smile because she prefers to be alone, even aloof. She had difficulty reaching out to and engaging people, and tended to be judgmental about her students. I wanted her to learn to smile. The ritual itself involved the use of water for purification of the mind, speech, and body—touching water and bringing it to the eyes, lips, and heart. This was the act of bringing Christ into the heart, feeling Christ there. While chanting from Indian tradition, with each inhalation Christ entered, and there was a mantra in Catalan: "You are my breath, eyes, heart, body, speech/be within/be my strength in everything."

I've asked this student about the feelings that come from this worship, and she says it is an emptiness followed by a fullness, that there are instants of clarity that cannot be brought back into the patterns of thought and speech. I've noticed that when she brings student groups to Chennai she is now far more open and easygoing with them, enjoying her students more. She is a better teacher.

In *sutra* II.46, Patanjali teaches that *asana* must have the dual qualities of alertness and relaxation. This is exactly the quality that we must bring to meditation, or *dhyanam* as it is called in the *Yoga Sutras.* The primal condition is to *be there,* to be in a place in which all obstacles that might distract body and mind have fallen away. We are prepared to direct the mind (*dharana*) toward a chosen object. The question now arises, what is the chosen object?

Many heads have rolled over whether to meditate upon a form or the formless—and I don't wish mine to be among them. Yoga actually resolves this issue. In our tradition, we view the form as founded upon the formless, an expression of it. As a practical matter, my father taught that it is easier to begin with the form that ultimately will give way to the formless that lies beyond.

Since the mind is incessantly active, it proves helpful to engage a question in meditation. It is like a line cast by the intellect that helps focus it. This can be done in conjunction with a physical image or object—although the object must be fairly simple. In the young Catalan woman's case, for example, it was Jesus's smile that was the object, and her quest was to answer the question, "Where is the smile within me? What is the nature of the smile, its source in Christ?"

A symbolic design can also be used, and even the simplest can reveal the power of consciousness to open up, to explore, to expand. For example, a square divided into four squares can have various meanings, interpreted according to the individual or to cultural associations. It can represent two opposite forces, two opposing elements. In Japanese calligraphy, it signifies that when two forces join together, we are rich. Numerous other meanings can be found in the symbol.

Patanjali laid down the principle in the clearest terms: the object of meditation influences the meditator. It is for this reason that we must be prudent and discriminating in our choice of questions and symbols for meditation. We are engaged primarily in a profound process of self-study, the quest to "know thyself."

This brings up another aspect of meditation. What is the role of the ego, the "I"? Students from the West, in particular, seem to have a burning desire to get rid of the ego. It is often construed as a narrow self-absorption, fueled by fears and desires of external origin, or as an urge to inflate one's sense of self. In these interpretations, "ego" can indeed seem to be an obstacle. But such a concept of "I" has no place in the teachings of Patanjali.

The great sage is very specific on the role of "I" in *dhyanam.* In describing every aspect of mental activity, he states that even when you have something in front of you, you may not see it. Conversely, even when you don't have something in front of you but you want to see it, you will see it. Everything depends upon *you.* You may think you have a question when in reality you don't; or you may not have a question but will find it as well as the answer in the course of meditation.

According to Patanjali, comprehension is dependent upon two things: (1) The interest and force of the *purusha,* which directs the mind toward an object, and (2) the proximity of the object. Without interest, there is no question, no answer—the object remains invisible. To the motivated mind, borne along by faith, anything can be revealed. I remember a striking example of this. Once, my father had been performing *puja* and meditating, when he suddenly called out to me to come at once. "Look there!" he said, pointing at an image representing Vishnu. "Can you see? The God is here, His eyes are glowing." I did not see it, but my father did. As he bore witness, such is the process of meditation from confusion to discrimination and clarity, from the gross to the subtle. Without the "I," how can such a process occur? Without the "I," what can we bring to the supreme union?

Another way to understand this process is the movement from what we hear, see, or learn from authoritative sources such as scriptures; to the beginning of understanding; to true perception—seeing the fire itself, the reality, the truth. Without this progression—for example, when you take a guru's word for authority because it suits your fancy—mere acceptance of truth will not make it valid for you. The "I" must undertake the movement: the "I" must find truth for itself. So, the three aspects necessary and present in meditation are the intellectual, the reflective . . . and something else. All of which leads not to the elimination, but rather comprehension of the "I."

There is an aspect of Yogic practice, including all those leading to *dhyanam,* that cannot be overemphasized. As we bring our meditation to a close, perhaps with chants and ritual, we must do so in a way that prepares us for the next phase of our life. The businessman who performs *aradhanam* described his purpose in meditation so admirably. It was to preserve his sanity in the maelstroms of the modern international business world. When my father exited from his rituals and meditations, that was often the moment when he would begin to write poetry, his mind and spirit open to pure creativity.

On the other hand, rituals and meditation can also be used as a refuge from life, a way of trying to avoid problems and anxieties, and this can be distinctly to our disadvantage. I knew an executive who was having terrible troubles with both his family and his business. He went to his astrologer, who advised him on the influences of the zodiac and how to deal with them. Then, he went to his priest who prescribed all the necessary sacrifices and prayers to perform to remit his errors and remove sin. Still things didn't improve, so he went back to the astrologer, who told the man how he had misinterpreted his response, and then he went to the priest who told him he must have erred in the performance of his *puja.* And so it went. If the unhappy man had devoted some of the time, energy, and money spent on astrologers and priests to his real problems in his career and family, he might have solved them.

Any journey has a starting point, a place of arrival, and the effort to bridge the gap between. What kind of journey will it be?

We're familiar with going about errands in our car. Usually, we allow for the expected obstructions and delays. Traffic is heavy and slows us; we hit all the stoplights, and perhaps there are accidents or even an unreasonable policeman who scolds or gives us a ticket. The air is heavy with exhaust fumes and the noise of vehicles and horns jangle in our ears. Nearing the destination, we find ourselves driving around the block or many blocks in search of a parking place. We arrive, at last, with nerves on edge, temper frayed, and energy drained. A commonplace experience.

Rarely, something quite different happens. We leave the driveway and it seems as if everything is designed to speed us on our way in the most carefree fashion. Traffic flows; we only encounter green traffic lights. Without deviation we arrive at the shop we want and miraculously there is a parking place waiting for us right out front. (I assure the reader that such an occurrence is indeed a miracle in Chennai!) We can't escape the feeling that we must be doing exactly the right thing, at the right time, in the right place—even that there are invisible hands helping us along the way. A most un-commonplace experience!

And yet, what is the real difference? The second trip that I have described was, of course, somewhat easier, somewhat quicker—all the external conditions seemed to favor us. The reality is, despite the external conditions, we achieved what we intended, what was necessary. That the usual journey was more difficult really makes little difference in the outcome. It was the same driver, same vehicle, same starting point and arrival. What made all the difference was not the difficulties encountered, but how we responded to them. There is no reason why our first journey to the shop should not have left us feeling just as clear-minded, good-tempered, and energetic as the second.

The analogy illustrates the basic purpose of Yoga—to bring to our lives quality of action, quality of thought. We might call it the goal of *living accurately*. This is the starting point for our efforts to go beyond what we know. First, we must understand and respond appropriately to the known. In this striving we may draw upon the lessons bequeathed to us in ancient texts such as the dialogues of the *Bhagavad Gita* and the *sutras* of Patañjali.

The *Bhagavad Gita* is, above all, a practical teaching to Mankind, and it is very much about *dhyanam*—not as meditation seated in front of a symbol or as an act of worship. It is the interaction with what is happening at the moment, our response to it, and our attitude about that response. The central theme of the *Bhagavad Gita* concerns *dharma*. This is usually translated as "duty" but in fact resonates with meanings that pervade every aspect of our lives.

Prince Arjuna is faced with a terrible crisis: he must go to war with his friends, teachers, and members of his family. Everything inside of him cries out against inflicting pain and death upon them, even to wishing death for himself. Yet his *dharma* is very clear, as Lord Krishna helps him to understand. Arjuna is a warrior, his place is on the battlefield to defend what is right. He and his brothers had exhausted all other means of seeking redress for the wrongs done to them. His vow to avenge an insult to his wife, his oath to his king, and his own mother's approval and urging all combined to define unequivocally that this fight was an act of *dharma*.

Krishna's guidance is to help Arjuna remember his real nature, which has been forgotten for an instant. Step by step, Krishna leads the warrior prince through his doubts, his emotional storms, and his confusion to the truth. Each of these steps is a meditation:

- Upon what one must do, how it should be done, and what is the right attitude toward this action;
- Upon knowledge: What is conscious, what is not conscious, and what is Ishvara, the higher force;

- Upon detachment: that which must be forsaken, and that which should never be forsaken.

The dialogue moves to the highest plane, in which Krishna invokes *bhakti*—the surrender of our will and actions to God:

Abandoning all duties, come to Me alone for shelter.
Be not grieved, for I shall release thee from all evils.

The *Bhagavad Gita* is not about the virtues of war, nor is it a myth or ancient history. My father spoke of it as a very new book, describing the immediate, recurring, and epic struggles of everyday life. Modern man and woman—and child, too—confront so many challenges and difficulties in striving to fulfill the many different roles of work, family, school, community, culture. With this, there is also the progression of the individual mind and spirit that must be part of a fulfilled, joyous life.

All the resulting obligations and conflicts—physical, mental, and emotional—are now usually lumped together under a single, forceful term: *stress.* Science recognizes it as a threat to health both as a cause of disease, and as an obstacle to recovery. Since none of us is free of it, we also recognize stress as life-draining, an enemy of well-being and happiness.

Though Yoga has many solutions for the symptoms of stress, they are only symptomatic solutions. We can remove tension through *asana* and calm the emotions with *pranayama.* Myriad other possibilities exist, ranging from massage to aerobics classes to hitting a golf ball—or a punching bag. The stressful symptoms will be removed for a while but will soon reappear. With Yogic practice, once the symptoms subside an individual must examine himself and search for the cause of the problem.

In our tradition, stress originates in two attitudes: "I am the doer" and "It is for me." These attitudes underlie *avidya,* the obstacles to clear perception, which Patanjali described as misapprehension, confused values, excessive attachments, unreasonable dislikes, and insecurity. And these in turnlead to troubling emotions expressed as desire, anger, possessiveness, self-delusion, arrogance, and envy. In practice, the outcome invariably is *dukha*—the constraints upon our physical and mental life that lead to illness and discontent.

We might note that Patanjali made one of the wisest, stress-reducing observations ever. We must never feel guilty or ashamed about experiencing the *avidya-dukha* cycle. It is as fair and universal as death itself, visited upon each and every one of us. Within the *Bhagavad Gita* and Patanjali, we also discover the means of ultimate liberation from the cycle.

To effect change in our lives is a process of progressive linkage of the mind, a replacement of less desirable associations of the mind with the more desirable. Yogic practice can be reduced in essence to this all-pervading concept of linkage. We begin with the *conscious* linkage of body movement and breath, of *yama* and *niyama*—our relations respectively with others and ourselves. At this point, we have already achieved much of what my father spoke of as the purpose of Yoga. With proper diet and continuous practice, we begin to achieve health of body, clarity of mind, and the ability to communicate and to relate on other levels with those around us. Already, much of the stress in our lives is reduced. But we can progress further.

As we continue our practice, we begin to see the possibilities of higher linkages of mind and spirit. The role of the senses and our emotions becomes more apparent. On the basis of self-reflection; we see how they tend always to draw us back into old patterns, into old grooves of thought, action, and response. This is based on experience, such as, "I have failed before and probably will again." We can displace this condition and replace it with something more positive. To do this, we need to introduce into our study two indispensable elements of change.

The first is called in Sanskrit *svadharma. Sva* means "self," and *dharma* is that which protects, holds up, and elevates. In the upholding of *dharma,* every person has a role to play. We each have responsibilities, and we must be very clear about what each responsibility entails, and do our best to discharge it. It is also necessary to be clear about the limits of this responsibility and not to interfere in, or worry about, things that fall within the orbit of another's responsibilities. This distinction between what is ours, and what lies beyond our responsibilities is *svadharma.*

The second element is *shraddha,* or faith. There is perhaps no greater difference—I am speaking in the broadest terms—between the cultures of East and West than in our attitudes toward faith. The Western mind has been so pulled toward liberation and autonomy that faith has acquired a connotation of unreason, the irrational. To the Eastern mind, there can be no faith without reason. In a conversation with the Dalai Lama, his Holiness put it so perfectly: "Blind, unquestioning faith in a person or an ideology, without reason and analysis, will eventually lead to disaster." Only direct personal experience takes us beyond reason and analysis toward faith as acceptance.

Recognizing our responsibilities and intentions, and pursuing them with faith is the guide for linkage that takes us to ever higher levels of experience. But we still must be free of those two attitudes which, as I've mentioned, are the root causes of stress, of *avidya-dukha:* "I am the doer," and "It is for me." This is progressively displaced by the attitudes: "Not by me," "Not for me."

In both the *Bhagavad Gita* and the *Yoga Sutras,* the highest linkage is surrender to and union with Ishvara. But there is a crucial difference. In the "divine song," Ishvara signifies Narayana, the supreme God; in Yoga, Ishvara is given to us as the supreme teacher, the all-knowing, beyond error. Because of this distinction, the Vedanta school of thought rejects Yoga as godless. Because of this distinction, Yoga is compatible with every religion and philosophy. Yoga is neutral, the threshold beyond which each individual chooses his own doorway to the highest power. Acceptance of this highest force, in Patanjali's teaching, is called *Ishvara pranidhana*—meditation upon, linkage with, and absorption into Ishvara.

I taught my first seminar on meditation a month after my father's centenary celebration, to a group of students from the United States and Europe. At the close of two weeks of sessions, my father came to the seminar and accepted a single question from a student: "Upon what should we meditate?" Krishnamacharya smiled at the group, and said: "*Ishvara pranidhana.*" That was all he said, or needed to say.

In describing this process of ever more positive linkages, I don't wish to suggest that it is a continuous, smooth, effortless path. Quite the contrary. Patanjali is rife with warnings about the nature of the obstacles we encounter. The senses and our feelings are constantly drawing us back to previous patterns of thought and action. Also, the mind and its capacity to form linkages is unpredictable—except for the fact that it is always attaching to something. It is essential to understand the nature of linkage in itself.

Linkage is not necessarily a matter of guided direction and attraction. We are often most powerfully linked to an object by struggle and conflict. Smoking is a perfect example. Sri Aurobindo, a famous guru who founded a community south of Chennai, shocked many of his devotees by smoking cigarettes. His followers from the West were especially distressed.

"How can you, a Yogi, smoke when it is expressly forbidden?" they would ask.

He responded: "Yes, I'm attached to cigarettes. But you are attached to non-cigarettes!" Of course, Aurobindo continued to smoke.

Again, many are troubled by sexual desires and attachments. My father was very clear about this. He taught that even with what we feel to be undesirable attachments, we must first draw closer to them. We must understand and experience them, and only then can a true process of change, of making the effort to displace a former linkage with a more desirable one take place. Caution is necessary. We must be very careful about what we deem to be desirable and undesirable linkages: such discrimination is a never-ending task of self-study.

The peculiar power of linkage was brought home to me during my early visits to the West when I began to read about Christianity and to discover what a magnificent religion it is. I was always baffled, though, by Saint Paul. How was it that this Roman official, so fanatical in his persecution of Christians, became the apostle whose teachings provide so much of the foundations of Christianity? It happened, of course, when he was blinded by a vision of Christ on the road to Damascus. Still, it seemed to me strange that such a total transformation should take place. Then, I remembered the Hindu parallel.

Ravana was the great enemy of Lord Rama. Ravana hated the god with all his heart, all of his life and efforts were dedicated solely to harming and destroying Rama. Yet, when Ravana was finally killed, he went straight to heaven! Why? It is because his heart was constantly filled with thoughts, feelings, and words about Rama. He was constantly linked to the god. Those who are one with God always enter heaven. Similarly, Saint Paul as a persecutor always had his mind filled with thoughts and feelings about Christ. At the moment of transformation, each enemy of God became that with which he was united—even though the uniting force was hatred.

To repeat, we must be very careful about the nature of our minds' linkages. They can have the most unexpected results.

Dhyanam, or linkage with the object, has in the instances I've described moved to the level of *samadhi,* complete absorption in and union with the object. There is no longer a distinction between "I" and the object of meditation. This level of meditation is most readily observed in the works of artists.

A few years ago I was in Italy, invited to give a talk in a beautiful church in Florence. It was an interesting occasion. The bishop in charge of the church was chain-smoking and very anxious because the insurance people had told him no more than 250 were permitted to attend, and far more were crowding through the doors. As for myself, I was at a podium in front of a large oil painting of the Last Supper. I wasn't at all uncomfortable, but it did seem odd that a Hindu was giving a talk about Yoga in a Catholic church while standing in front of a picture of the Lord's final communion with his disciples. What made the greatest impression was the painting itself. I don't remember the artist, but I was overwhelmed with the beauty, feeling, and meaning of his work. It was an act of profound meditation: at the highest level, *samadhi* manifests as creativity of the highest order, beyond what we think of as humanly possible.

Among many instances, I also witnessed this power in the work of a good friend of my father's. She was one of India's most famous dancers, and when she came to visit him she was very old, so crippled with arthritis and injuries that she could barely walk. Yet, when she took the stage and the music began all the infirmities fell away. She danced like a young girl, like a goddess. I remember my father asking her how she was able to do this. She replied, "When I dance, I think of Lord Krishna. He fills me, takes over. There is no pain. Only the dance." My father said to her: "You are a great Yogi!" It is the only time I ever heard him say that to anyone.

Meditation is not only evident in the creation of works of art. It is equally present in our relationship to them, how deeply we can enter into the artist's act of creation. All artists I've known whose works surpass anything we've known before invariably ascribe the source to a higher force, whether they call it God or not. The work then becomes an object for our own contact with something higher. In the course of my teaching, I've learned that I can assess the level of anyone's practice of meditation by the way they relate to artworks, to music—and to other people.

In everything I have described about Yoga, there are two common threads. There is the fact that everything we do, at every level of practice, is infused with conscious involvement—from the simplest movement of an arm to contemplation of a work of art. We always bring our mind to the experience.

There is also the experience of flow, inward and outward, to everything we do. There are the contracting and expanding postures of the body; the inhalation and exhalation of the breath; the bringing of an object of meditation into our hearts and minds, and our flowing back into the object until we are one with it. Perhaps we might view our lives in the same way, as one long, single experience of the breath.

We take our first, faltering gasp of air the moment we leave the womb. We draw life into us in the early years of childhood, youth, and early adulthood as we learn, discover our nature, find our place in the world: our *dharma*. In its fulfillment, we begin to give back all that we are capable of, all that we can offer to others. As a long expiration, we gradually give back this breath of life and consciousness, returning it to the source, to God. My father's death had this quality of gentle return.

Four months after his one-hundredth birthday celebration, Krishnamacharya began slipping away. I was with him as much as possible; he continued to teach, to pass on all that was possible. Four hours before he fell into his final coma, he was reading and marking up a Buddhist commentary that he wanted me to read. After he lost consciousness, we took him to the hospital—and as his blood pressure dropped, the doctors said he would be more peaceful at home. At all times, there was chanting by his bedside. I was with him when he released his final breath. I'm told people usually gasp at the end, but my father's chest only rose and fell, rose once more and then subsided. That was all there was. He passed easily from life. When we moved him from the bed, we found under his pillow bank notes worth five thousand rupees. No one had known the money was there, and it was precisely the amount needed to cover the funeral expenses. Even in death, my father refused to be under obligation to anyone. It was Krishnamacharya's final act of independence.

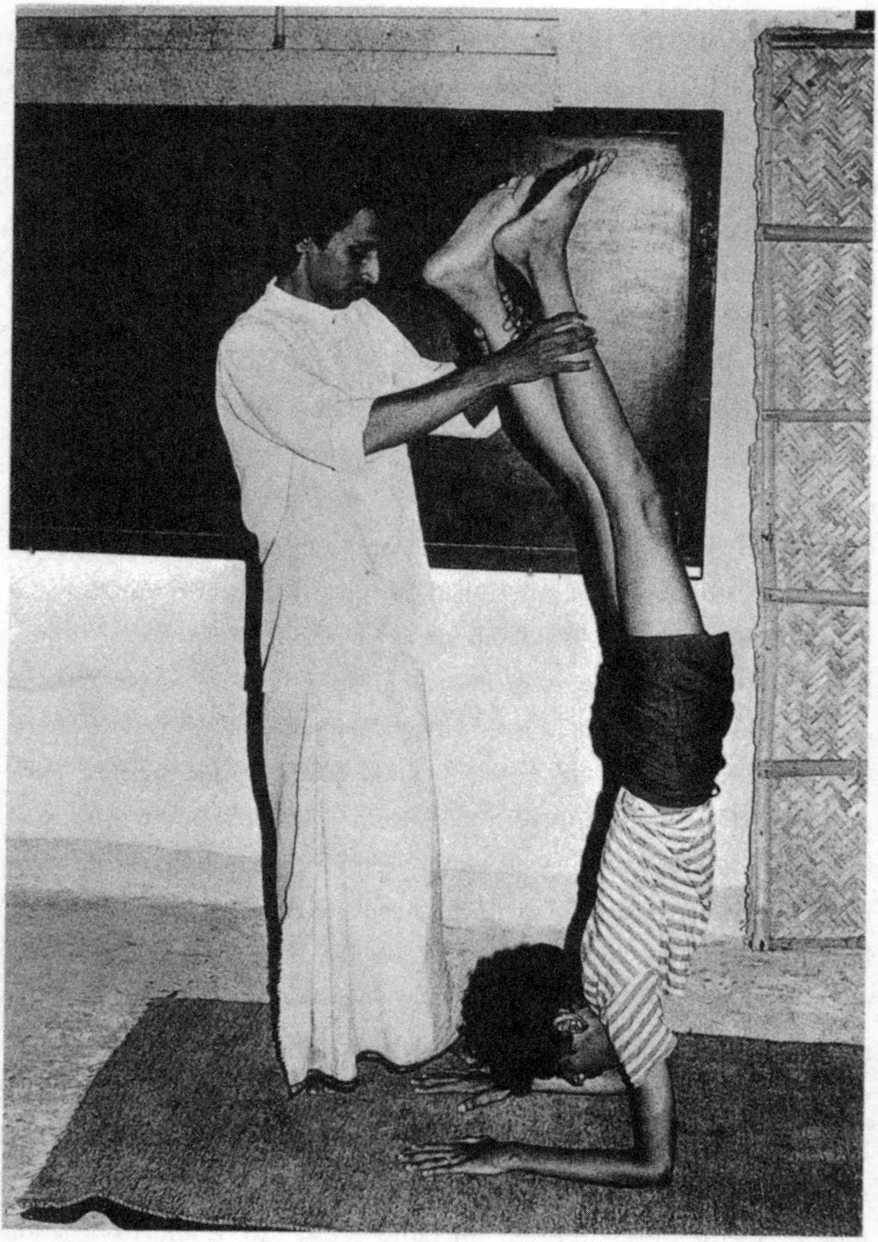

Teaching Pinchamayurasana *at the Krishnamacharya Yoga Mandiram, Chennai, 1984*

CHAPTER EIGHT

TO BE A TEACHER

Teach what is in you.

Not as it applies to you, to yourself,

but as it applies to the other.

Four years after my father's death, I set out with three American friends on the most ambitious pilgrimage of my life. Our destination was Mount Kailash and the sacred lake, Manasarovar, in the Himalayas of western Tibet. The mountain is the abode of Lord Shiva, who gave Yoga to humanity, and the lake is the place where my father had arrived eighty years earlier to begin his profound studies of Yoga with Sri Ramamohan Brahmachari, the guru who taught Krishnamacharya in a cave for seven years. We were also headed for the region where lies the source of the Ganga, known in the West as the Ganges.

From droplets in ice caves, from tiny rivulets, and from seasonal floods and melting snow, this great and holiest of rivers begins a wandering, twisting course through northern India that culminates in the Bay of Bengal. Barely discernible at the beginning of its journey, the Ganga takes on a force that becomes irresistible, that has laid waste to cities and monuments of the past. The Ganga is also ever-renewing for the land

and people along its path, and for the spirit of India.

We are all familiar with the ancient saying, "You can never step into the same river twice": everything is always in a state of change. It is equally true that wherever you step into a river, you are always bathed by the river. Whether you step into the Ganga near its origin, from the banks of a tiny village, or at one of the cities along its route—Allahabad, Benares, or Calcutta, for example—you become part of the timeless flow of the Ganga.

It is the same with that enduring stream of knowledge known as the *parampara.* Wherever we make contact with the lineage of teachers—from reading or chanting the works of the ancients to a class in a modern city—we touch upon the entirety of that wisdom.

Paying homage to the source of inspiration in our lives is irresistible to those who understand, perhaps instinctively, the nature of pilgrimage. For me, the journey to western Tibet was to honor my father's memory, and also to renew my sense of belonging to the teachings of his *parampara.*

Krishnamacharya's death was a great sadness to his students and friends and, even more so, to our family. My children were especially close to him: they were his best friends at the end of his life. My elder son, Bushan, shared his grandfather's devout religious temperament; Mekala, my daughter, played music on Krishnamacharya's *veena* and, to his delight, had covered his notebooks with her drawings. My younger son, Kaustubha, always sought out his grandfather for comfort and advice when he was troubled—or in trouble.

As a man in his fifties, my sadness at the loss of a father was perhaps eased by maturity and accepting the inevitability of the death of a man who had lived one hundred years. As a teacher, however, I felt—and continue to feel—Krishnamacharya's death quite differently. There is an English word that I like, "go-between." Within the family, I had often been the go-between for my mother or sisters when something had to be taken up with my father. For thirty years, I had been the go-between linking my students to Krishnamacharya. Whenever there was a problem or new challenge, I could always take it to him. I was very happy to be a good go-between. And then, Krishnamacharya was no longer there to consult as readily as before. This loss I felt very deeply, and I wanted to feel closer to his presence. Where better than his own source of inspiration and wisdom? Despite the difficulties, we set out for the place where, as Kaustubha describes his grandfather, Krishnamacharya became "a go-between between man and God."

Our party consisted of Dr. William Skelton, a composer and professor of music, who had been a student of my father's; his wife, Mary Louise, who had studied with me; and a physician, Dr. Craig Wilson. I always saw Bill and Mary Louise annually because we had worked out a program of Yoga studies at Colgate University in upstate New York. The seminars for students alternated between Chennai and Hamilton, New York. The results of several of these seminars had been edited by Mary Louise and John Ross Carter into a book, *Religiousness in Yoga: Lectures on Theory and Practice,* which is a fairly detailed exposition of concepts and techniques.

Bill, too, had made wonderful contributions to our work. He had arranged a grant for me to publish an introduction to Patanjali's *Yoga Sutras,* a translation and commentary. It was based on my father's teachings, but when several thousand copies arrived in Chennai, as arranged, I was very unhappy with my effort. Somewhat to the horror of teachers and students of the Mandiram, I lit a fire and burned each and every copy. Bill not only wasn't dismayed, he was very supportive. He refused to accept my attempt to refund the several thousand dollar grant. Instead, he urged me to use the money for another attempt, which led to a far more satisfactory work published by Affiliated East-West Press Private Ltd. Bill never even mentioned the bonfire.

Our first stop was Kathmandu in Nepal, in part so that Bill and Mary Louise, who were in their mid-sixties, might adjust to the higher altitudes. My preparation consisted of climbing the stairs at home fifty times each day—a wonderful exercise. After decades of *pranayama*, I found the altitude caused no difficulties.

We had embarked on an unusual route. Because Mount Kailash and Lake Manasarovar are so sacred to Indians, the Chinese government permitted a limited number of pilgrims to visit from a destination in northwestern India. People were taken in buses and, for me, it seemed altogether too much like a guided tour. Also, I wanted very much to see Tibet and to meet its people. Fortunately, it was one of those periods of relative political calm, and so we were able to fly from Kathmandu to Lhasa on a Chinese airline that served a substantial meal and also thoughtfully provided vials of medicinal herbs designed to help adjust to the altitudes.

In Lhasa, our first destination was the Potala, the traditional palace of the Dalai Lama. As gifts, we brought the monks photographs of his Holiness, who lives in exile in India. These images are now forbidden, but at that time we were able to see how very much they meant to the people of Tibet. The monks had so much respect for these photographs that they would not even look directly at them.They placed the images on their heads.

The deep-felt religious experience of the monastery, where young and old, man and woman, pauper and high official worshiped equally, was so beautiful that we wanted to chant within it. We asked permission, and mentioned that since we were going to Mount Kailash we wanted to chant in worship of Shiva—to recite his 1,008 names. With greatest courtesy, we were shown to a room in the monastery and as soon as we began, a monk entered and brought us tea. Imagine: strangers in one of the most sacred Buddhist monasteries made welcome to chant from the Hindu Vedas. In how many temples of the world's other religions would such tolerance be found?

We left Lhasa in two all-terrain vehicles with Chinese drivers and a

Tibetan guide, and quickly discovered that the main road was impassable because of two collapsed bridges. This proved to be a stroke of luck. It meant that we would have to find our way along "paths" that were mostly indistinguishable from the rocky rubble of the terrain. We saw a landscape seldom traveled by outsiders: valleys at 14,000 feet with mountains towering nearby; freshwater rivers flowing into huge salt lakes; hot and sulfur springs driven forcefully from beneath some of the rivers, and the fantastic geological variety of the country. Many of the rivers we simply drove through. Our drivers would check the depth and current by tossing in stones, which wasn't very reassuring. So, we had Craig, who is an excellent swimmer and surfer, walk through first to see if the vehicles could make it.

After twelve days of camping, we came to Kailash, which is like no other mountain of the Himalayas. A high projection rises between two peaks, each with a distinctive profile: one side reflecting brilliant sunshine off its snowy surface, the other pure white. Here, we left the traditional offering of stones to the goddess. Testament to centuries of pilgrimages were the millions upon millions of stones left by worshipers at Mount Kailash and Lake Manasarovar.

At the lake, we were at first disappointed because there seemed to be no caves. The slopes of the mountains were either too muddy or too hard and rocky. Then, Craig and I spotted on the northern side of the mountain what appeared to be the ruins of a monastery. We climbed up and found a patch of land, where herbs might have been grown, and an ancient grinding stone. Instinctively, I felt that this was the place where my father had lived. It was here that he had learned Yoga in a way that is different from the many other forms of Yoga that are taught. Krishnamacharya's Yoga is based upon absolute respect for the individual, absolute devotion to the infinite potential within each of us. It is Yoga that is always practical in matters of body, mind, and spirit. And, of course, I was fully aware that this was the place where the guru had instructed my father to go into the world and be a teacher of Yoga—the place where his destiny was decided. Later, I undertook the ritual clockwise progress of fifteen miles around Lake Manasarovar. We camped there for three days, a time for prayer and meditation, and then made our way back to Chennai.

What is the pilgrim's experience? One of the best explanations I've ever heard was given, in a different context, by one of my earliest students and oldest friends, the Belgian teacher Claude Maréchal. Claude began studying with me twenty-five years ago, and today he is one of the foremost teachers of Yoga in Europe. He has trained a generation of accomplished teachers who are now training the next generation. Each year, Claude leaves his family and work in Liège and visits me in Chennai. I asked him recently, "Claude, why do you keep coming to Chennai? It's a difficult trip and there's nothing more I can teach you." He answered, "I come to strengthen my sense of responsibility. And to lighten it."

I believe that is one of the most original and accurate descriptions possible of the relationship between student and teacher. It is a bond that lightens as it strengthens.

In previous pages, I have touched often upon this relationship. It is a sustained one-to-one encounter essential to the progress of an individual in Yoga. Equally, it is the most difficult condition for many to grasp—or to accept. The reasons are understandable.

In the West, many sensational stories have circulated in recent years about notorious gurus from the East who attract throngs of fanatical followers. They dress in different clothes, leave family and friends behind, change their names, and seem to offer the guru mindless, slavish devotion. We read stories of sect leaders surrounded by bodyguards with weapons, even as the guru lives in luxury fit for a maharaja. How can this be possible?

With respect, I suggest that it is because so many people in the West live with so much anxiety and stress. Despite all their progress, prosperity, and comforts, they live with constant dread, often coupled with unsatisfied spiritual yearnings. Along comes a man with a white beard and flowing robes from exotic Asia who says "I have all the answers!" People turn to this self-proclaimed guru from sheer relief, from a desire to shed all the difficult responsibilities of life. In India, we've had many centuries of experience with such "gurus"—and millions of us, too, are just as gullible. I am not referring, of course, to the great spiritual teachers who emerge from time to time, but only to the few who exploit. Sadly, they have instilled an understandable suspicion about placing trust in a true guru, a true teacher.

The questions to be answered are among the most frequent that I'm asked. What is a true teacher? How will we recognize him or her? What is our responsibility, as student, to the teacher? What can we expect from this relationship?

My knowledge is based upon the experience with my own teacher. But I know of no one who has ever expressed the student-teacher relationship more eloquently than Mala Srivatsan. In February 1996, we held at the Mandiram an unprecedented meeting, hosted by Aperture Foundation, that included some of the world's leading practitioners of healing traditions. Represented, among other disciplines, were Ayurveda, Tibetan and Chinese medical systems, Anthroposophy, modern neuroscience, and, of course, Yoga. I asked Mala to speak to the gathering about my father, and these were her words:

> It is very difficult to express feelings that are so personal. My experience with Krishnamacharya has been so immensely powerful, so immensely beautiful. It was in 1980 when I met him first. He had gone through this evolution of experience himself. He had become an *acharya*, which means many things—including one who has traveled far. He had practiced and taught, and taught what he practiced.

I had a lot of complications. It was not only asthma, but also strong pain due to sciatica. From my experience with my *acharya,* I feel there has to be another energy that comes not from our own system, but from their blessing. It is more important than the energy you can feel in the physiological system.

When I met Krishnamacharya, I was twenty-two years old. From the time I was an infant I had been treated on and off with antibiotics, periodically with steroids. I then met someone who said, "Why don't you go see this old man who teaches Yoga?" Being brought up in this culture—in this environment—we do have faith in our own system. So, even though my own university education had been in rationalist, Western psychology, I did go to him with a lot of faith.

The first thing that Krishnamacharya said when he saw me was, "I can help you. I can cure you. But you have to do all that I ask you to do. Are you willing?" The first request of the teacher is surrender. You let him take over rather than you deciding what is good, what is right. If you cannot accept the surrender, I think you decide your destiny. Something in me made me feel I could do what he asked. That's where our relationship began.

There were a lot of dietary requirements . . . many dos and don'ts. He would give me his own medicines. He said, "No taking of steroids or any other medicines." At that time, I was on steroids every day. I didn't ask any doctor's advice. I simply did what my *acharya* said. For the first few days, he would ask me to come and sit beside him. He examined me thoroughly, taking the pulse at different parts of the body. The way he would communicate, the way he made you feel was that you were so important, creating the feeling of wanting you to be healthier. It was miraculous. Within a week I stopped wheezing. I feel he was able to

> influence the student with his own energy. He didn't need even to touch you: no *asanas* or *pranayama* or anything. I did not start any practice for the first week. I would just sit with him. He would change my diet for that day. How can you describe this kind of person? The only thing you can say is, extraordinary!
>
> Slowly, over the next few weeks, he did put me on some *asana* and *pranayama* practice. There was such a drastic change in my physiological system. Only people who've gone through it can understand what it's like—to stop wheezing after a lifetime of it.

I don't want anyone to think that Mala is completely cured. Her asthma and sciatica come and go, but it doesn't matter. She is capable of living life so fully, and of giving so much to her family, to her teaching . . . to the continuation of my father's work. Nor do I want anyone to feel that, to study Yoga successfully, they must find such a perfect teacher-student relationship. It is very rare. But within Mala's reminiscence, we find essential elements that help in our own quest for a teacher. From that, and from my own experience as student and teacher, let me offer some suggestions.

A teacher of Yoga should live a life of Yoga—to practice what is taught. There can be considerable confusion about this. To begin with, to live a life of Yoga is about continuous practice and self-study. This is not a question of style. Like all individuals, teachers of Yoga will exhibit every conceivable kind of personality, temperament, and human problems. They experience failed marriages, personal suffering, and stress. They do not all go around in Indian dress. Nor—despite what Europeans in particular seem to expect—are they always calm and serene. I've often been asked, "Aren't Yoga teachers supposed to be free of emotions?" My response is simply, "Take a look at my family!" With a wife and three children, including two teenagers, I assure you that our house is as filled with all the emotional joys and storms of any other "normal" household.

A good teacher of Yoga also is not necessarily someone who can perform all manner of complicated *asanas*. In fact, some of the best teachers I know, because of physical problems, cannot even sit cross-legged comfortably. To live the life of Yoga, to repeat, is about a faith that continuously guides the teacher toward practices leading to the harmony of body, mind, and spirit.

From this it follows that the teacher must be motivated in part by self-interest—not selfishness but enlightened, generous, self-interest. Krishnamurthi was once asked, "Why do you teach?" He answered: "To find out what I know," to which I might add, "and to find out what I don't know."

The bond between teacher and student is like a rope between two mountain climbers. The less experienced climber behind can ascend no further than lead climber makes possible. I like this simile because it also suggests the absolute bond of trust that must exist between student and teacher. The more a teacher advances, the more he or she can give to the student.

Even as a teacher is urged on by self-interest, his or her entire responsibility is to the student. The most fundamental commandment of Krishnamacharya is that only the student matters, and the teacher is there to help that individual evolve according to his or her own unique situation and potential. There is no standard, no conformity in this approach. There is no will to bend a student toward the teacher's ideas or purpose. In this sense, the teacher is like a mirror, but unlike any that simply gives off a two-dimensional reflection. It is a mirror that reflects from all directions, through time, extending into relations with others, and that most especially reveals the action of senses and emotions upon the mind.

The teacher must always speak the truth. This, too, must be comprehended fully. The truth spoken must never be harmful to the student. It must be expressed according to the student's needs and ability to grasp the meaning. As I've said, my father and I went painstakingly through the *Yoga Sutras* seven times. If at the beginning he had taught what passed between us later, it would have made little or no sense to me. Yet, we were going over the same eternal aphorisms each time. I've talked with my brother about Krishnamacharya's lessons on ritual and discovered that he taught each of us in entirely different ways. The teacher must be acutely aware of what needs to be said and what it is possible for the student to hear. But there must never be a lie, only truth.

Finally, and this is by far the most important, the teacher must care more about the student than himself. This is a matter of the heart, not the intellect. I know of individuals with brilliant minds and an enormous knowledge of Yoga who cannot teach. It is not in their hearts. This is not a harsh judgment because they are well-meaning, and they also have much to contribute, for example, in research or publication. We are each unique, which means that the caring so necessary to the teacher will not be the same in everyone.

For the teacher, only the student matters. And the student is never wrong. I always know when there is trouble with teachers. It is when they start complaining about their students.

And so the qualities we seek in a teacher are a life devoted to practice; evidence that he or she, too, is ever a student of Yoga; a nature that is always truthful; a commitment to the student's own awareness and possibilities, each in his own terms. And caring—above all, caring. When people arrive at the Mandiram and ask us, "Can you help me?," the only response we can ever make is "I can care."

And what of the student? What does he or she bring to the encounter?

The first task of the student, obviously, is to decide whether or not to seek out, and then to accept a teacher. Already, a process of self-study is engaged, and there are many people who cannot bring themselves to such acceptance. Not many will immediately be filled with the faith that Mala placed in my father. For them, teaching will be found in reading texts, meeting well-informed masters and the like. For the student who is capable of engaging in a more profound relationship, it helps to begin with listening to the teacher, perhaps reading his or her works, or attending a class or two. The student should carefully consider the personality and the approach. Is this teacher too severe, too soft—or as I've described these qualities earlier, too *brmhana* or *langhana*?

Whether or not the student is accepted depends upon the teacher, but the decision to seek the teaching is entirely the responsibility of the individual. It is a decision that should not be unduly influenced by another.

Once the decision is made, however, the student should not hesitate. The time for inquiry and exploration is over. The commitment must be made completely. After all, the study of Yoga is a gradual, continual, often difficult progression, and this cannot occur without the powerful underpinning of commitment.

The student must accept the teachings as taught. Here, too, there is enormous misunderstanding. I am not talking about mindless absorption of another's thoughts and ideas as one's own. That is of no value because there is no comprehension based upon experience—no *living* what is taught. With proper respect and humility, a student should be able to raise any question. I was able to ask my father anything, provided I raised the question with respect—and he was in a suitable mood. Also, to accept teaching does not necessarily mean to agree with it. I don't agree with everything my father taught. And Krishnamacharya disagreed with the teachings of some of the greatest authorities in the history of Yoga.

Before we know to question, to agree or disagree, we must first understand what the teacher is offering. In Yoga, this further means to engage practices we are taught, whether physical, mental, or spiritual. Only through accepting the *experience* of the teaching can we know if it is of value to us. It was only because my father accepted and fully comprehended the lessons of his teachers that he was able to adapt and change their knowledge for the present and future.

The student is responsible for his or her own learning. If I do not understand what my teacher says, then I must look to my own failings first. The effort, with its successes and failures, is totally mine. It is also true that the student may find it necessary to leave a teacher, to reach a point where it is best to seek another. What is to prevent it? To repeat, the responsibility to learn is the student's.

Finally, the student owes the teacher courtesy and respect. Humility in this sense is not having a low opinion of oneself, but being free of arrogance and pride. The absence of respect for the teacher in all forms of education is far more than a breach of etiquette; it is a serious impediment to learning.

To sum up, the student must bring to the teacher a willingness to undertake great effort and even risks; to arrive at an unhesitating decision to accept the teacher; to accept what is taught, and to take responsibility for his or her own learning. And the student should respond to the teacher's selfless caring with a proper attitude of humility and respect.

The qualities of the teacher and of the student, as I've described them, may sound old-fashioned. In truth, they are ancient prescriptions, laid down thousands of years ago, which endure because they are so effective, so practical.

And what is the experience to be found in this student-teacher relationship? What can we expect of it? There are no guarantees, but there is a natural process.

The Sanskrit term *samskara* describes, in effect, the patterns of our lives. These are the physical and mental habits, the past conditioning, the relationships and obligations that keep us, it seems, going around in circles like a needle stuck in a groove. Each of us exists in a state of *samskaras,* and they can be to our detriment or to our advantage. We can become caught in cycles of failure, distress, and conflict which become the recurring themes of our lives, which govern our life experience. Or we can engage *samskaras* rich in challenge, in productive work, and in service to others.

The purpose of the student-teacher relationship is the constant evolution of *samskaras* to ever higher levels of consciousness and action. It is the progressive refinement of our ability to observe and alter the power of the senses, the emotions, and external influences over our minds. The teacher is necessary because it is so difficult to observe ourselves. The ever-present *avidya-dukha* cycles cloud perception. With the care and guidance of the teacher, however, we learn to enlist the senses and feelings as the instruments that lift us to ever higher *samskaras.*

If we complete the work, the end result, as Patanjali describes, is liberation from all *samskaras:*

> *When the mind is free from the clouds that prevent perception, all is known, there is nothing to be known . . . the three basic qualities* [gunas] *do not excite responses in the mind. That is freedom. In other words, the Perceiver is no longer colored by the mind.*

For many who pursue the religious path, the hoped-for destination is union with God. As Patanjali states, in concert with the message of all the great religions, this is ultimately beyond human will and effort. Only God decides—a matter of grace.

To the extent that it lies within human effort, however, Yoga can help prepare the mind for this divine encounter, or, indeed, for the fully realized experience of life. Krishnamurthi, so often critical of religions and religious practices, rather surprisingly called it the "religious mind." To quote my late student, teacher, and friend for a last time:

> A religious mind is a young mind, which is a mind that is learning and therefore beyond time. Only such a mind is a religious mind, not the mind that goes into temples, that is not a religious mind.

> Not the mind that reads books and quotes everlastingly, moralizing. That is not a religious mind. The mind that says prayers, that repeats, repeats, is frightened at heart and blind with knowledge . . . therefore it is not a religious mind. The religious mind is a mind that is learning and therefore a mind that is never in conflict at any time and therefore a young mind, an innocent mind.

What a wonderful prospect! The body may be irrevocably destined for aging, decay, and death—but the mind can be ever-renewing, ever young.

With some understanding of the necessity and value of the student-teacher relationship, the question inevitably arises: How do I find the teacher that I need? I can't give any conclusive answer because each individual's needs are different. I can offer some advice.

Be willing to trust yourself. The instincts that awaken a yearning for Yoga are excellent guides to the teacher. Again, it is a matter of self-knowledge and one's own interests. Some will begin with a desire for a healthier, more supple body; others, with a keen interest in meditation or philosophy. What is important is to make a beginning somewhere, with someone—and then to be guided by one's own inner wisdom.

I will also emphatically urge a prospective student to *look nearby!* It is not necessary to travel to India or to find a teacher with a lengthy Hindu or Tamil name. Yoga is India's gift to the world, but we do not own it. I'm constantly baffled by people who think we do. A typical example occurred not long ago when a young foreign woman came to the Mandiram. I talked with her and knew that the best possible teacher for her during a brief stay was a New Zealander who has studied with us for several years. He is not only a good teacher, but also a writer, lecturer, and editor who has helped increase awareness about Yoga in his own country. The young woman tried a couple of lessons, then came to me and insisted that she must have an Indian teacher. We provided one, who was not nearly as effective. She could have made far more progress, but left satisfied that she had studied Yoga with an Indian *Yogi*.

Any student is likely to gain more, particularly in the early stages, with a teacher who comes from the same culture, the same traditions. Already there are so many common points of reference. Consider how many Sanskrit terms and concepts that the reader has had to wrestle with in the pages of this book, which is purely introductory. And I've exercised as much restraint as possible in employing them. From direct experience, I know that there are many excellent teachers in the West.

It is said: to the earnest student the teacher will appear. It is impossible to be more specific, but in my experience it is nearly always what comes to pass.

I've dwelt upon the importance of the teacher not solely because it is a subject so essential to the study of Yoga. There is a more personal reason. I know that all of the effort and genius of my father's lifetime of work and devotion will survive only in the persons of the teachers who continue his tradition. The training of teachers is, to me, of equal importance with the teaching of students at the Mandiram and elsewhere. We might have devoted our resources, which have grown over the years, to beautiful buildings and grounds. Perhaps we one day will have a building of our own, but we remain in the same two-story, thatched-roof structure I rented years ago. It is far more important to devote every effort, every contribution to the creation of new generations of teachers.

The living tradition of Krishnamacharya is embodied in those who understand and teach the freshness and vitality of one of the most ancient of all systems that lead to knowledge of the human condition—and freedom from its limitations. It is an ability to comprehend the ancient wisdom of Patanjali and the *Bhagavad Gita* as if one is hearing them at the moment of divine revelation. It is also about an openness and a courage to undertake any change needed to preserve and renew this ancient wisdom for the benefit of modern man and woman.

Toward this great work, my father made profound contributions. He would reject that statement because he attributed all of his works to his guru and to God. Krishnamacharya placed his immense learning utterly at the service of Yoga, the service of Mankind. He eliminated barriers that prevented women from forms of study and worship, and insisted upon the absolute equality of anyone's right to the full fruits of Yogic study. He set what I believe are unparalleled standards of tolerance. Difference never meant incompatibility to Krishnamacharya, and any student of any belief—including the most passionate of atheists—was welcome to study with him. All he asked for was sincerity of purpose.

Most of all, though, I believe that my father's greatest contribution was in his selfless devotion to the individual—to the possibility of unimaginable growth and freedom that is inborn in each of us. This, for Krishnamacharya, was the gift of Yoga and the hope of Mankind. It was expressed so beautifully in a poem that he wrote. I excerpted a stanza from it at the beginning of this book. Here is the poem in its entirety, as rendered in the original Sanskrit and its English translation, with my father's salutation to all who read it:

from *Yoganjalisaram:*

SHLOKA 1

Oh, sleepy mind,
Praise Lord Krishna, remember the God of Knowledge.
Pray to the Teacher,
For, when the body becomes weak and depleted,
Your education will not save you.

SHLOKA 5

Knowing for sure that all the objects you come
into contact with are impermanent,
Do not get lost in them, instead,
Again and again resolve to be aware of the Eternal Self.

SHLOKA 6

Where is the conflict when the Truth is known,
Where is the disease when the mind is clear,
Where is death when the breath is controlled,
Therefore, surrender to Yoga.

SHLOKA 10

Man desires objects when tender in age,
Enjoys them when young,
Seeks Yoga when middle aged and
Develops detachment when old.

SHLOKA 13

One who is deeply absorbed in God and with a firm mind
Salutes Him with all his heart, receives everything he desires,
And the Lord smilingly asks,
"What more do you need?"

SHLOKA 21

Regular Yoga practice steadies the mind;
Regular chanting develops initiative and intelligence,
Unwavering meditation results in extraordinary benefits,
And the repetition of Mantra helps in self-realization.

SHLOKA 26

Speak the truth that is pleasant,
See everyone in the light of friendship,
Remove the body of its toxins, and acquire
The best of education, humility, and wealth.

SHLOKA 32

Regulate the breath.
Be happy and link the mind with the Lord
in your heart.
So reveals Yogi Tirumala Krishna,
As a message for humanity.

योगाउवलिसारम्

śloka 1

गृणु गोपालं स्मर तुरगास्यं
भज गुरुवर्यं मन्दमते।
शुष्के रक्ते क्षीणे देहे
नहि नहि रक्षति कलियुग शिक्षा॥

śloka 5

दृष्ट्वा स्मृत्वा स्पृष्ट्वा विषयं
मोहं मा कुरु मनसि मनुष्य।
ज्ञात्वा सर्वं बाह्यमनित्यं
निश्चिनु नित्यं पृथगात्मानम्॥

śloka 6

ज्ञाते तत्वे कस्ते मोह:
चित्ते शुद्धे क्वभवेद्रोग:।
बद्धे प्राणे क्वास्ति मरणं
तस्माद्योग: शरणं भरणम्॥

śloka 10

रागो भोगो योगस्त्याग:
चत्वारस्ते पुरुषार्था हि।
बालस्तरुणो वृद्धो जीर्ण:
चत्वारस्तान् बहुमन्यन्ते॥

śloka 13

तव वा मम वा सदानुसरणात्
नमनान्मननात् प्रसन्नचित्त:
भगवान् वाञ्छितमखिलं दत्वा
किन्ते भूय: प्रियमिति हसति॥

śloka 21

नित्याभ्यसनात् निश्चलबुद्धि:
सतताध्ययनात् मेधास्फूर्ति:।
शुद्धाध्यानात् अभीष्टसिद्धि:
सन्तत जपत: स्वरूपसिद्धि:॥

śloka 26

वद वद सत्यं वचनं मधुरं
लोकय लोकं स्नेहसुपूर्णम्।
मार्जय दोषान् देहप्रभवान्
आर्जय विद्याविनयधनानि॥

śloka 32

बन्धय वायुं नन्दय जीवं
धारय चित्तं दहरे परमे।
इति तिरुमल कृष्णो योगी
प्रदिशति वाचं सन्देशाख्या म्॥

योग:- चित्तवृत्तिनिरोध:।

Yogaḥ - Cittavṛttinirodhaḥ

Statue of Patanjali in the Courtyard of the Krishnamacharya Yoga Mandiram, 1987

EPILOGUE

Throughout recorded history, the pursuit of happiness is Mankind's abiding quest. It is the underlying theme of mythic tales, of historic sagas, of literary creation. One nation, the United States of America, was created in the belief that the pursuit of happiness is an "inalienable right." Expressed in one form or another, the search for happiness inspires virtually all religious practice.

The happiness we seek is more than that which is felt in momentary experiences such as the joyous laughter of a child, the fulfillment of a desire, or the victory over an adversary. What is sought is more than the absence of misery or sorrow, more than solace.

We seek happiness everlasting, and all of the world's great religions offer hope and guidance toward its realization.

India's great gift to humanity is an accessible, practical approach to an enduring state of happiness. This is the gift of Yoga. It is a gift offered to individuals of all beliefs, denied to none who wish to receive it.

The revered scriptures of ancient India take a very sophisticated approach to the search for happiness. They prepare definitions, classifications, and methods appropriate to each individual. Taken into account are personal interests, vocation, age, sex, family, social position, and cultural setting. There are detailed descriptions of proper attitudes toward the self and others: of when to act and when not; when to speak, when to be silent. The pursuit embraces freedom from suffering, an end to the fear of dying, life beyond this world, and union with the Absolute.

The methods are numerous, the permutations so limitless that each individual may discover what is uniquely suited to him or her. Yet the primal truths are simple.

The path to happiness is a revelation of God as granted to a few of humanity's most inspired seekers. Their greatness lies in the fact that they transmitted this wisdom not as aloof scholars, but as individuals who knew the harsh trials and challenges of the human condition. They labored, persevered, and won their way to the truth and its rewards. They are guides along a journey that leads from our most immediate, mundane experience into the realm of transcendent mystery.

The pursuit of happiness is a journey toward God. It is a journey of the mind, inseparable from body and spirit.

Impossible is a perfect definition of God. Countless millennia of attempts to endow a Creator with names, images, and attributes have inspired the chants, hymns, prayers, meditations, artworks, and other expressions of longing and worship that are among Mankind's own divine creations. God is ultimately considered as the source of all that exists, immeasurable, beyond any desire, the most powerful, the all-knowing, the all-giving, the Teacher. Beyond comprehension, God is yet within our reach.

The mind, too, eludes exact, final definition. Yet, the mind is within our grasp. The mind is the primary instrument for achieving all human ends, including happiness. Yoga is both the art and the science of perfecting that instrument.

The Yoga of Patanjali, as taught by Krishnamacharya, bases the labors and journey of the mind upon three fundamental premises:

- Each individual is absolutely unique, endowed with a universal capacity to achieve union with God.

- Everything in creation is reality.
- Everything changes, and is subject to change through the mind's capacity to comprehend and to shape action.

While simply stated, these premises may well require a lifetime of effort to develop the mind that truly masters their meaning.

Consider the uniqueness of the individual. Even in societies that apparently cherish the idea, the overwhelming cultural pressure is to establish norms of conformity and expectation. Society, family, and media combine to set standards of success or failure. Acceptance or rejection depends upon set rules of behavior and speech. The individual is constantly pulled away from his sense of uniqueness—for example, by the exalted standards demanded of an astronaut, or by peer pressures that lead our children into self-destruction. Even as we say aloud "uniqueness of the individual," we recognize how little we can hear, let alone understand what these words mean at the deepest personal level.

From the viewpoint of some religions and philosophies, the statement that "everything is reality" is not only a departure but in some cases even heresy. In Yoga, we assign real existence to the intangible as well as the tangible—to the fleeting impressions of the mind, to the senses, to memory, to imagination and dreams. Belief has real existence as do its variants, including skepticism and nonbelief. The premise of an all-embracing reality reveals the ancient sages' wisdom of experience, and the practical nature of Yoga. For the mind can approach, focus upon, and ultimately comprehend perfectly all that is real. How can we relate to, let alone involve ourselves with what is not real, nonexistent? It is through these encounters with reality that the mind conducts its journey. Along the way, nothing is denied, nothing lost, nothing wasted.

The realization that everything is subject to change may be the greatest obstacle to happiness. We welcome those changes that bring moments of delight and satisfaction—the birth of a child, the recovery from illness, financial gain. Yet, even in these moments, we sense movement. Change takes away the beauty and energy of youth. At peaks of health we know that we will again experience injury or illness. Possessions acquired through wealth can be lost or lose their power to gratify. Change always seems pointed toward a sense of loss, inevitably of life itself.

And yet it is precisely in this understanding of the inevitability of change that the meaning of Yoga enters our life and beckons toward happiness.

This is Yoga as the progression into the new.

"Yoga" is a word freighted with definitions, as evidenced in all the previous pages of this book. Perhaps the most important have to do with the ideas of "progression" and "new." This is the ancient meaning: "To move from one situation to another; to understand what I have not understood; to gain that which I lack."

The movement is in itself Yoga. Like all journeys, there must be three stages: (1) The place where we begin, (2) the choosing of our destination, and (3) the effort to arrive. It is not an easy journey. Difficulties, frustrations, and disappointments will arise. We are likely to falter. That is why it must be a movement of continuous effort and gradual progression. Always, it is movement into the new, into the previously unknown and unexperienced. And it is in this progression that we undertake the most sublime of human adventures, a path of discovery toward true and abiding happiness.

The particular circumstances of our place of beginning are unique to each individual. But since we are embarked on a journey of the mind, we each begin with the effort to understand and to master how it works.

The mind receives input from the senses and initiates action: we read to the end of this page and turn to the next. When the senses provide inadequate information, the mind draws upon stored data: we recall from previous reading a reference that enhances comprehension. Even when no information is available from the senses, the mind is able to function on the basis of authoritative statements: we don't know the meaning of a word and so consult a dictionary. Even when nothing concrete exists, the mind can create imaginary forms: immersed in reading the Bible, we conjure up pictures of Jerusalem or experience dreams in which an image of Jesus or Mary appears.

What the mind comprehends is not always accurate, with or without the input of the senses. Too many influences—such as past conditioning, desire, fear, and ignorance—are at work upon it. This fact is crucial to the beginning of our journey. Once we examine the source and nature of our misapprehension, we begin to liberate the mind for true comprehension. We gain the ability to act at the right time, free from error. In this effort, the second phase of our progression can be most helpful: choosing our destination.

Long ago, the ancients recognized that the mind can be developed to focus with enormous power in a particular direction. When the mind is so directed it can achieve virtually anything. What we can aim for in Yoga is limitless. Restored health, improved intellect, enhanced athleticism: we can set our sights on lowering blood pressure, solving a mathematical problem, or becoming a winning tennis player.

If happiness is our goal, there can be only one direction for the mind and that is toward God. To do this requires faith and ardor, as well as the continuous effort needed to keep the mind from drifting away toward lesser or distracting aims.

Again, the ancient sages reveal their practicality. They recognized that the mind takes only the form presented to it—and that it can create forms based on words and images. In this way, the idea of devotion emerged. If we can use these forms to relate to a perfect being, we may approach this perfection. The words and images we employ must be supported by faith. The deeper the faith, the stronger the image. Faith is the sure knowledge that we can and will succeed. To strengthen our faith, the ancients taught that everything we see and experience has a cause. Just as all brothers and sisters are born from common parents, so everything we see in this and other worlds has a common source. The source is God, the seed of all that is created or will be created, possessing infinite knowledge of Creation. All originates and is resolved in God, selfless in the guidance and care of all seekers.

There is one extraordinary difference between God and Man. Lacking nothing, God has no defenses, sets up no barriers against Man. It is Man who erects the defenses and barriers against God. In their removal is the happiness we seek.

How is the journey of the mind, the pursuit of happiness, to be conducted? As we raise this question, we must thoroughly understand that the mind is inseparable from body and spirit. Yoga brings body, mind, and spirit into ever greater harmony, and so the journey toward happiness is above all about deeply felt and conscious experience. And just as we know the journey consists of three stages—beginning, direction, and effort—its conduct also has three elements: Practice, study, and openness.

Practice is action. In this, Yoga differs from—without excluding—other schools of philosophy and of belief that rely solely upon intellectual inquiry or presumed truths. Yoga always incorporates felt experience and so, for many, practice begins with the most basic functions of life: movement, respiration, and nourishment.

In Yoga, consciousness enters and merges with movement into prescribed exercises, the *asanas.* The body moves toward a balance of relaxation and alertness. Consciousness enters and merges into the inhalation, retention, and exhalation of the breath in *pranayama.* We move toward understanding that something greater than "air" constantly flows through us. Consciousness enters into the choice and quantity of food we eat. We move toward nourishment as the source of invigoration, not satiety.

Even with such basic practices we experience that a threshold is crossed. They give us each day a measure of time for ourselves. It is time enjoyed in a relatively neutral manner, free of distracting, disturbing thoughts. These practices improve our health, appearance, and sense of well-being. They are the most readily accessible means toward self-awareness: consciousness of the source, the nature, and the consequences of our actions.

With equal commitment we undertake those actions that define our relationships with others: Our capacity for truth, enriching communication, and caring. We replace envy for those who are more successful with joy for their accomplishments; in place of contempt for those who are weaker or less successful, we feel compassion. Such actions not only enhance our relations with others, they also free us from shackles that have restrained our own development. We bring consciousness toward further actions of benefit to ourselves—to our surroundings, work, relaxation, and sense of contentment.

The second element necessary in our journey toward happiness is *self-study*.

Yoga teaches that everything placed before the mind is a mirror: the mind takes the shape of what is perceived. For modern man and woman, that mirror is progressively a window upon electronic images from elsewhere—the computer or television screen. While not intrinsically wrong, such imagery possesses a power to numb and pacify as well as to awaken and stimulate.

Self-study engages the action of the mind. It can be accomplished by the study of texts; by closing the eyes and chanting, prayer, or meditation; or by seeking out and engaging the company of the gifted, the elderly, and the wise. From the experience of others—through the spoken or written word—we may find the example and wisdom that lead to our own self-discovery and inspiration.

The third element—and the most important—is *openness*. Since we are embarked upon a journey into the unknown, it is obvious that we do not know all that we need to know, that we do not always act in the best possible way to attain our ends. If we were perfect, there would be no need for progression. To be open is to accept two truths. First, we accept, deep within ourselves, that we might be wrong. Second, that we can always find the way and means to change.

Beginning, choosing a destination, and then undertaking it may be viewed as three successive stages of our journey of the mind. Yoga teaches that the three elements needed to conduct it are to be engaged at the same time. To achieve our goal, we must bring practice, self-study, and openness into the regular pattern of our lives. Like mind, body, and spirit, they are inseparable in the progression into the new.

We need something more. We need the teacher or teachers who will help us along our way. No one seeks to excel at anything without the help of a teacher: the music student learns from the master musician, the athlete from the best coach, the bricklayer from the craftsman of masonry. We accept the need for teachers in these situations as a matter of course. How much more important, then, is finding and accepting a teacher who can help shape the immeasurable richness of our lives.

In the search for a teacher, Patanjali offers implicit guidance. We know that the teacher of Yoga will live the life of Yoga. We know that he or she will be capable of almost superhuman caring. We know that the teacher will be both giving and selfless—a guide who will help us in the direction of independence and personal autonomy, not servitude. Finally, we know that the teacher, too, is beyond any concern but union with God.

It is true that a very few individuals are born into a state of Yoga. They need no teachers, although they are not always beyond succumbing to the snares and attractions that can diminish their endowments.

Curiously, those born with effortless comprehension are seldom very good teachers themselves. They seem to lack the experience of, and empathy with the human condition. Lord Krishna of the *Bhagavad Gita,* the

Buddha, the law-giver Moses, Jesus Christ, the prophet Mohammed—each experienced profoundly the sorrows, pain, trials, questions, and ultimate bliss that mark the human journey toward God. As a result, they are among Mankind's eternal teachers and also exemplars of the qualities we seek in our contemporary teachers.

Our relationship with a teacher helps awaken the power of healing within us. Healing is a matter of relationships, whether it is the healing that aids the recovery from, or management of an illness, or the healing—the making whole—that leads to the harmonious union of body, mind, and spirit. And in the continuing progress of our Yogic experience, each of us will understand both the benefits and the necessity of becoming a teacher to others. It is part of the learning and part of the sharing incumbent upon a journeyer toward God.

Even as ancient sages guide us along the progression into the new, their voices from the remote past sound with warnings. The journeyer has known distractions, frustrations, and disappointments. Through faith, which sustains his actions and study, he has persevered. When obstacles arise, his willingness to be open to change, and to undertake it in a spirit of freshness and ardor sustain him. Now, he approaches the final and greatest hurdle in the pursuit of happiness.

Despite the clarity and powers he has acquired, it dawns on him that he is not—he cannot be—the master of everything. There is a greater intelligence, a greater force. The existence of God is recognized and he yearns to find God. He seeks guidance and begins to pray. His attitude toward money, possessions, career, family—all change: God is seen in all of them. He finds a sudden relief. His senses do not run away or distract from his chosen direction. Health is there, not as an end but as a means to pray, to reflect, and to act, and his actions are without attachment to the results. As clarity develops, he begins to accept that there is more than can be seen, the apparent cause is not the real one. The play of God in the universe is evident and immediate.

When this new awareness develops, the journeyer finds himself in an elevated position compared to others. He possesses more clarity, more depth, greater vision than those who are materially better off. He can see what others cannot. His actions seem more efficient and less of an effort. He ages more slowly and appears more attractive. His presence attracts others and he is seen as one who can help and guide: he has the ability to control events. He is not betrayed by past conditioning, memories, or imagination. His potential gives him great power, enormous possibilities. But if he yields to the power and the possibilities he is trapped. He loses hold of himself. His acceptance of a higher force, of God, is replaced by the presumption of his own apparently extraordinary self. Rather than union with the absolute, there is appropriation of the appearance of godhood.

This crucial self-encounter, like the pursuit of happiness, is also an underlying theme of myths, epics, and great literature. It is the moment that precedes tragedy or triumph.

If the error is not recognized in time, the journeyer experiences a fall from the threshold of grace—a fall of his own making. It is a continuous regression, all the more agonizing because he once knew better than others the true possibilities of his existence.

If the error is recognized and acted upon, it is the final and greatest of lessons. Through renewed effort, the journeyer again approaches and is absorbed into his all-powerful source and guide. His life is now full but empty: full of hope and caring for others, empty of desires for himself. A life of unimagined devotion, service, peace, and patience ensues.

It is the rare individual who will complete the journey to happiness, and each man or woman who undertakes it will experience it in a unique way. But it is open and accessible to all. And even for those who do not progress all the way, there is more happiness to be found in the striving than in all the attachments and material rewards of common existence. And there is also a belonging in the perfection of God—an undeniable belonging, even if our perceptions are dimmed to it, of union with the Absolute. This is the revelation for all humanity, from the most profound depths of the Upanishads: the primal Sanskrit teaching:

> *Tat Tvam Asi: "That thou art!"*
>
> It is the affirmation of God to Man.
>
> *Tat Tvam Asi: "That thou art!"*
>
> It is the recognition among Mankind of
> the Godhood in each of us.
>
> *Tat Tvam Asi: "That thou art!"*
>
> It is the acceptance of, and surrender to
> God by Man.
>
> *Tat Tvam Asi! "That thou art!"*

AFTERWORD

Yoga is one of India's greatest gifts to mankind. It is a science that has relevance to the atheist as well as to the seeker of God; it is unconnected to any particular religion, and is applicable to all of humanity.

Humans are always in search of happiness, even without knowing what real happiness is. The chaos and complexities of life can make us feel miserable. Through his study and practice of Yoga—a science almost as old as civilization—Krishnamacharya revealed one path to human happiness, to the tranquillity of mind that is the source of happiness.

Keep the body strong and healthy, keep the mind serene and calm—these are the philosophies of Yoga. It is an ancient system, conceived by the saints and sages of India, and codified more than two thousand years ago by Patanjali Muni in a collection of aphorisms called the *Yoga Sutra.* This collection is the basis upon which the practice and philosophy of Yoga have developed over the centuries. Many great minds have been applied to the *sutras* in an effort to discover the secrets hidden in them—but merely reading (even many times) will not bring those secrets to light. To come to an understanding of the *Patanjali Sutra,* reading must be backed by intense practice.

Krishnamacharya was perhaps the greatest modern exponent of the *Patanjali Sutras.* Not content with his own realization of the truths in the *sutras,* Krishnamacharya supported institutions where others could learn and practice Yoga; his aim was to train hundreds of teachers so that the great message of the *sutras* could be spread throughout the world.

Krishnamacharya's son, T.K.V. Desikachar, was originally trained as an engineer—and had begun a successful career in that field—but chose to give up engineering to become an intimate disciple of his father's. Desikachar had the benefit of living with his father for many years, listening to his talks, and, most importantly, observing how he lived as a practitioner of Yoga. An accomplished teacher himself, Desikachar founded in Chennai the Krishnamacharya Yoga Mandiram, where men and women come to learn to practice Yoga and have a healthy life. Many people are also trained here to become Yoga teachers; students come from all parts of India and abroad to take advantage of the Mandiram's training program, and to carry the message of Yoga to various parts of the world.

I am sure that *Health, Healing, and Beyond* will be welcomed among Yoga students and teachers throughout the world. I congratulate and give my good wishes to Desikachar for his continuing service to humanity through his Yoga Mandiram, which I hope will continue to grow as a truly international center of research and development of Yoga.

— C. Subramaniam
Chairman, Bharatiya Vidya Bhavan, and Elder Statesman

ACKNOWLEDGMENTS

The support, encouragement, and shared experience of scores of individuals in India, Australia, Europe, and the United States contributed to the making of this book. Leslie Kaminoff originally proposed the collaboration between Sri Desikachar and Aperture, and provided helpful advice during the course of the three-year undertaking. Diana Stoll was the most devoted of editors. Among many others whose contributions are gratefully acknowledged: In the United States: Juan, Kathryn, and Noah Levy, Pat Massey, Dr. Barbara Nylund, the artist Wendy Cadden, Sonia Nelson, Martin Pierce, Anne Rogers, Phyllis Honemann, and Ann Zeller. In Belgium: Claude Maréchal. In France: Pierre Courtejoie, Hoda Khoury, and Michel Nicolas. In Germany: Martin Soder, and Imogenn Hannah Dalmann. In New Zealand: Mark Whitwell. In Switzerland: Malek Daouk. In the United Kingdom: Nick Waplington. In India: His Holiness, the Shankaracharya of Kanchipuram; the hospitable priests of Alvar Tirunagari; Mr. M. M. Murugappan; Dr. B. Ramamurthi; Mr. A. V. Balasubramaniam; Mrs. Jaya Krishnaswamy of the Madhuram Narayann Centre for Exceptional Children; Dr. and Mrs. R. Ramasubramaniam of the Shrsti Foundation, Madurai; J.P.S. Pattabhi Jois. Particular thanks are due to the faculty, staff, and students of the Krishnamacharya Yoga Mandiram who gave unreservedly of their time and effort to this account of the life and work of Krishnamacharya. In this, they honor the memory of the *acharya* and further his tradition of selfless dedication and devotion to the well-being of others.

BIBLIOGRAPHY

The Bhagavad Gita, translated with introduction by Juan Mascaró, New York: Penguin Books, 1962.

Blau, Evelyne, *Krishnamurthi: 100 Years*, A Joost Elffers Book, New York: Stewart, Tabori & Chang, 1995.

Brunton, Paul, Ph.D., *A Search in Secret India*, New York: E. P. Dutton & Co., Inc., 1935.

Dhyansky, Yan Y., "The Indus Valley Origin of a Yoga Practice," *Artibus Asiae*, Vol. XLVIII, ½ (Ascona, Switzerland, 1987), pages 89–108.

Classical Dictionary of Hindu Mythology and Religion, Geography, History, and Literature by John Dowson, Calcutta: M.R.A.S., Rupa & Co., 1989.

"Shri T. Krishnamacharya: La Traversée d'Un Siecle," *Viniyoga*, No. 24, Claude Maréchal, ed., Liège, 1989.

The Encyclopaedia Britannica, Eleventh Edition, Cambridge, England, 1911.

Desikachar, T. K.V., *The Heart of Yoga: Developing a Personal Practice*, Rochester, VT: Inner Traditions International Ltd., 1995.

Desikachar, T. K.V., *Religiousness in Yoga: Lectures on Theory and Practice*, Lanham, MD and London: University Press of America, 1980.

Patanjali's Yogasutras: An Introduction, Translation and Commentary, New Delhi: Affiliated East-West Press Private Ltd., 1987.

The Yoga of T. Krishnamacharya, Madras: Krishnamacharya Yoga Mandiram, 1982.

Swami Vivekananda, *Raja-Yoga*, New York: Ramakrishna-Vivekananda Center, 1982.

Muthiah, S., *Madras Discovered*, New Delhi: Affiliated East-West Press Private Ltd., 1992.

Norman, Dorothy, *The Hero: Myth/Image/Symbol*, an NAL Book, New York and Cleveland: The World Publishing Co., 1969.

Eliade, Mircea, *Yoga: Immortality and Freedom* (translated by William R. Trask), Princeton: Bollingen Series LVI, 1969.

Hiriyanna, M., *Outlines of Indian Philosophy*, London: George Allen & Unwin Ltd., 1964.

Sargent, Winthrop, *The Bhagavad Gita*, Albany, NY: State University of New York Press, 1995.

BIBLIOGRAPHY